D. George Vanderlip

Discovering a Christian Life-Style

Guidelines from the New Testament

Judson Press ® Valley Forge

Unless otherwise indicated, Bible quotations in this volume are in accordance with the Revised Standard Version of the Bible, copyrighted 1946, 1952, 1971, 1973 © by the Division of Christian Education of the National Council of the Churches of Christ in the United States of America, and are used by permission.

Other versions of the Bible quoted in this book are:

The New English Bible, Copyright © The Delegates of the Oxford University Press and The Syndics of the Cambridge University Press, 1961, 1970.

Today's English Version, the *Good News Bible*—Old Testament: Copyright © American Bible Society, 1976; New Testament: Copyright © American Bible Society, 1966, 1971, 1976. Used by permission.

The New Testament in Modern English, rev. ed., Copyright © J. B. Phillips, 1972. Used by permission of The Macmillan Company and Geoffrey Bles, Ltd.

The New Testament in the Language of the People by Charles B. Williams. Copyright © 1965, 1966, by Edith S. Williams. Used by permission of Moody Press, The Moody Bible Institute of Chicago.

Library of Congress Cataloging in Publication Data

Vanderlip, George.
  Discovering a Christian life-style.

  Bibliography: p. 137
  Includes indexes.
  1. Christian life—1960-   I. Title.
BV4501.2.V35   248'.4   78-7922
ISBN 0-8170-0805-5

To
Janice, Susan, Patricia, and John

Foreword

The major focus of Christian discipleship must be on the nature and character of life. The attitudes and actions that characterize everyday living are ultimately the final test of one's true devotion to God.

Too often Christians have felt that their primary preoccupation should be with precision in theology and correct biblical interpretation, to the neglect of working out the implications in a Christian style of life. Indeed, one's roots should reside in soil made fertile by clear biblical and theological commitments, but the test of a tree's health is in the fruit it bears.

It is equally tragic that a sincere concern for Christian living has too frequently degenerated into a legalistic, negative kind of ethic usually far more determined by cultural factors or personal prejudices than by biblical revelation.

Christians need to be receptive to an informed and balanced biblical perspective with regard to the Christian life. We must be willing to wrestle with the significant and decisive issues confronting us today. But any attempt to apply biblical principles to current life-style problems takes courage. The ground that must be covered is filled with ambiguities and differences of opinion. While it is not an easy task it is a vitally necessary one.

D. George Vanderlip brings to the task a high level of professional competence as a biblical scholar and the courage to deal with difficult and controversial issues. The combination is crucial if questions of Christian life-style are to be grappled with biblically and honestly.

Today's serious Christian must go beyond the "rules and regulations" approach to life and consider the implications of faith in reference to those issues addressed in this volume. While it cannot be expected that everyone will agree with all the conclusions drawn, one has to respect the writer for his willingness to take a position, for his balanced approach, and for the care with which he develops the biblical framework from which application to living is made.

The complexities of contemporary life and the dynamic nature of biblical teaching rule out simple formula answers with respect to questions of Christian life-style. D. George Vanderlip renders an invaluable service in stating the questions clearly and in helping us to struggle with the kind of living that should result from our understanding of the Bible and our personal devotion to Jesus Christ.

Daniel E. Weiss
President
Eastern Baptist Theological Seminary
Eastern College

Preface

Jesus calls us to follow him into a life-style which will honor God and which will minister to our generation. What does such a life-style involve? That is what this book seeks to discover. I am indebted to the Reverend Harold L. Twiss, Managing Editor of Judson Press, for the suggestion that there was need for a book written for lay people on the subject of Christian life-style for today. In this study I attempt to interpret the Bible responsibly and then to apply its distinctive ethical principles to the pressing issues Christians face in the modern world. It is my hope and prayer that this book will encourage dialogue among Christians, and that through such sharing "we may be mutually encouraged by each other's faith" (Romans 1:12) and be strengthened to minister in Christ's name in the world.

To Mrs. Culbert G. (Duron) Rutenber I wish to affirm my sincere appreciation for her conscientious and untiring assistance in preparing the manuscript for publication. To Dr. Thorwald W. Bender I convey heartfelt thanks for several helpful suggestions while the book was in preparation. To Dr. Daniel E. Weiss,

President of Eastern Baptist Theological Seminary, I express gratitude for the writing of the foreword. Finally, it is my pleasure to acknowledge with genuine thankfulness the unfailing support and encouragement of my wife, Elaine. "Her husband . . . praises her" (Proverbs 31:28).

D. George Vanderlip

Chapters

Contents

1
In Search of a Christian Life-Style

Everyone is involved daily in moral decision making. Few people, however, have been faced with as serious a decision as Prime Minister Winston Churchill had to make in November, 1940. At that time he was told by British intelligence that the city of Coventry had been marked by the Germans for almost total destruction. This information had been obtained by deciphering messages sent in the German war code. The dilemma Churchill faced was agonizing. It was this: Should he evacuate the citizens of Coventry and thereby save thousands of lives, or should he keep this secret knowledge to himself in order that the enemy might not discover that their code could be deciphered? Was the knowledge of the code ultimately more valuable to Britain than the preservation of the population of Coventry?

How would you have reacted to this situation? What would you have done? Churchill decided to keep the secret knowledge to himself. Except for giving a standard alert to ambulance and fire-fighting units, he did not share with Coventry the grim knowledge he possessed. The bombers struck as scheduled on the night of

11

November 14, 1940. So devastating was the raid that the Germans began to boast that they would "Coventryize" every town in England.

Did Churchill do the right thing? The seriousness of the prime minister's decision staggers the imagination. When President Franklin Roosevelt was told privately about Churchill's verdict, he said, "War is forcing us more and more to play God. I don't know what I should have done. . . ."[1]

HELP IN MAKING DECISIONS

Fortunately most of us will never be confronted with moral decisions which will have such far-ranging consequences as this one. Yet none of us escapes ethical questions. Are there moral principles which can guide us when we are faced with moral choices? How does the Bible help us in this matter? Are there certain Christian values which can direct us when we face moral questions? This book has been written in order to discover moral principles which can aid us in our search for a relevant Christian life-style for our generation.

The Gospel as "Gift" and "Task"

Professing faith in Jesus as the Christ marks the beginning of Christian discipleship. It is, however, just that—"the beginning." Faith and works, commitment and obedience go hand in hand. Christ has died for us, and thereby God's love for us and acceptance of us has been shown. Through God's grace, revealed in Jesus Christ, we through faith have become new creatures in him; we have become God's "new creation." This tells us what God has done for us and what we have experienced. In the light of these facts, however, there follows a task for us to do. As "new creatures" we have come under new management. We are now servants to Christ and not to sin, selfish ambition, or secular values. We have said, "Jesus is Lord." That confession is a call to obedience and to service.

Few will quarrel with the above description of the "gift" and "task" of the gospel. More books, however, describe the gift than explain the task. What God has done, the Bible makes quite clear. In his love and grace he has sought us and opened the way for the forgiveness of sins and for fellowship with himself. The second aspect of the gospel is the task before us. This we call "Christian ethics." Christian ethics asks questions like the following: "How, then, are we to live?" "What are the followers of Jesus of Nazareth to do?"

Principles of Action Rather Than a Legal Code

The New Testament is full of practical counsel on how to live as Christians in the world. The instructions which are given do not amount to a legal code with strict advice covering all circumstances and situations. Broad principles for action are presented. We belong to God and not to ourselves (1 Corinthians 6:19-20). We are to do everything to the glory of God (1 Corinthians 10:31). We are to be imitators of Christ (1 Corinthians 11:1). Love is to be the Christian's primary motive in all relationships with other people (1 Corinthians 13). The Holy Spirit, God's gift to the church, is to be the inner guide for Christian behavior (Romans 8). Along with these broad, sweeping statements there are found practical everyday instructions which echo the traditional morality taught in Judaism, and at times the practical counsel given by the apostle Paul resembles the "dos" and "don'ts" of the ethics of Stoicism.

Christian ethics could therefore appear to be a mixture of traditional Jewish ethics and practical advice from contemporary secular expectations of the moral life, plus the distinctive added dimension that we are to do all things "in the Lord." For example, in Ephesians the traditional Jewish commandment to honor mother and father is expanded by such words. It reads, "Children, obey your parents *in the Lord,* for this is right" (Ephesians 6:1, italics added). The Pauline letters use the expression "in the Lord" some forty times. The old commandment is not done away with but is enriched. These words remind us that all of life is to be viewed in the light of the lordship of Christ, and all of it takes on meaning from this center and base.

What Is Distinctive About Christian Ethics?

Since the Bible has this mixture of the traditional with the radically new, and since much that is urged on Christians is not very different from the expectations of Judaism or from high ethical standards in secular society, we may well ask wherein Christian ethics has any uniqueness. Is there a distinctively Christian life-style? Does it consist in opposition to contemporary secular values? Does it involve a peculiar style of dress, an unwritten code of what we eat or drink, an abstinence from certain amusements, and so forth? All of these have been and are still held up as partial answers to this important question. If nothing else, the variety of answers which are given reminds us that this is a question over which Christians have long wrestled and for which there is no uniform answer.

The key to the distinctiveness of Christian ethics is not in the actions performed as such but in the motivation behind our actions. The little phrase "in the Lord," mentioned above, reminds us that the center of our existence, our point of reference, has been radically changed. What we do , we do as unto the Lord. Loyalty to him is the motivation for all we do, since we do not belong to ourselves but to him. It is not the action but the motivation and frame of reference in each case which makes a particular act an expression of Christian ethics. This is the distinctive and distinguishing feature of Christian behavior. As Paul wrote, "Whatever your task, work heartily, as serving the Lord and not men, knowing that from the Lord you will receive the inheritance as your reward; you are serving the Lord Christ" (Colossians 3:23-24). We shall return to this theme a little later in this chapter.

ALL OF LIFE UNDER THE CONCERN OF CHRISTIAN ETHICS

Modern men and women are searching to understand who they are and what their place is in the world. Can the Christian faith help in this quest? Christian ethics deals with more than personal piety and the behavior of individuals within the Christian community. Its proper focus includes our relationship to the world, and it is concerned with all the multiple and complex dimensions which that relationship may take. Its sphere is therefore as broad as human experience. No area of life lies beyond the scope of Christian ethics. Ethics is the science of moral duty. It seeks to discover the proper goals of human life and action. It studies the moral principles by which we are to live.

By Whose Standards Are We to Live?

Christian ethics begins with some important presuppositions. The end for which a person lives is not that person alone. Christian ethics builds on a theological foundation. It begins with a strong belief in God. The world was created by God. Humankind as God's creation finds its meaning, purpose, and destiny not in a human-centered frame of reference but in a God-centered one. The God who gives content to the ethical ideal of the Christian faith is not the God of the philosophers or a God created by human imagination. Christian ethics builds on its understanding of the God who has made himself known in history to Israel and to the church. He is the God who spoke through the prophets and apostles, but most fully in Jesus Christ of Nazareth.

As Christians we do not decide moral action without regard to the will of a sovereign creator God. God and not human logic must be the ultimate standard by which morality must be determined. Otherwise we end up with the situation described in critical terms by writers of the Old Testament who spoke of times when "everyone did what was right in his own eyes." That is another way of describing chaos, with everyone being a law unto oneself. In such a situation there are no standards and there are no laws to guide the individual in particular, or society in general.

Our Involvement in the World

While we are in the world, we cannot escape from the world. We have to live out our lives in the sphere of human society. God's kingdom has not yet been fully realized among us. Therefore our moral guidelines will be less than the ideal. Our actions need to be determined in the light of what is possible. This gives a very practical note to the whole area of ethics. The concept of escaping from the world into a monastery, as was common in the Middle Ages, was a nonbiblical and unrealistic attempt to set up two spheres in the world with two separate standards by which to live. One of the contributions of Martin Luther and of the Reformation was to point out the error of this understanding of Christian ethics. There are not two standards by which Christians are to live, one for the "religious," and the other for the laity. There is one standard, and we need constantly to ask ourselves how we can apply the

Christian ethic to the various situations in which our lives are cast.

The Relationship of Justification to Good Works

Christian ethics is not concerned with asking the question "How can I live so that I can please God and be accepted by him?" It begins rather with the doctrine of justification by faith and then says, "Since I am a new creation in Jesus Christ, how am I (in thankfulness and obedience to the one to whom I belong) now to live?" It is not a matter of doing good works so that we can be accepted by God. We were and we are sinners. We are accepted without our own merits through the grace of God. But that acceptance calls us to a new loyalty and a new obedience. We have a new Lord. To serve this Lord is not only our duty but also our pleasure. We delight to do his will because insofar as we walk in the Spirit, his will becomes our will. We serve not because "we must" but because "we may."

Discipleship as Obedience

When we speak of justification by faith, we mean more than a subjective feeling of dependence upon God, or of faith in any concept or religious idea we may choose. Such a general notion of faith too easily becomes a vague religious feeling in which each person puts such content as he or she desires without any reference to an objective standard. This the New Testament will not permit us to do. It speaks of faith in Jesus Christ. This faith implies trust and commitment to one who was an historical person and in whom and through whom God has made himself known. The record of that revelation has been given to us in Scripture. We have therefore some objective standard by which to determine what we mean by obedience to Christ. As faith must be bound to the object of faith, namely, Jesus Christ, so obedience must be bound to the teachings of the one who is declared by the church to be the Lord of the church. In Nazi Germany there were those who were called "German Christians." In this case the interests of the state overshadowed and overcame all other values. In such a situation the state becomes all in all and the lordship of Jesus Christ is ignored. The result is the loss of any objective content which can bring judgment to bear upon non-Christian values. This threat is ever with us and can come to us in a hundred different ways. For this reason constant self-examination is needed. We must challenge all systems by "the Word." The Bible, the tradition of the church, and the continuing guidance of the Spirit through the community of faith will all play their roles in checking error and in affirming Christian ideals.

The Motivation for Christian Action

We have said that what distinguishes Christian ethics from all other ethics is not the actions themselves but the motives behind the actions. We are to do all things "as unto the Lord." Obedience to the will of Jesus Christ is the determining factor in all our behavior. The end result of our action and the action of someone else who acts from humanitarian or even possibly from selfish motives may not be noticeably different. The framework in which Christian action takes place, however, is that of the lordship of Jesus Christ over our lives and over the world in which we live. Love, too, will be present. That love has its ultimate source in God. It is a love which comes as response to his love. We love him because he first loved us. It is God's love which is shed abroad in our hearts through the Holy Spirit. It flows through us to the world in need. Motivation is therefore a key factor in determining whether an action stems from Christian ethics or from some other source. Christian morality is concerned with something deeper than just the actions which we perform. It raises the issue concerning the drive, the motivation, the force which from within compels us to act in the manner in which we do.

No action can, of course, be judged purely on the basis of motives. Actions which are by their very nature immoral cannot be made Christian and moral just by claiming high Christian motivations. We can think of the atrocities committed in the name of Christ when "heretics" were tortured in the Middle Ages, or of the inhuman acts of the Crusaders against the inhabitants of Palestine. Such actions, which we would now judge critically on the basis of Christian morality, were not ultimately motivated by the high ideals of the lordship of Christ. They violated Christian principles which determine the morality or immorality of our actions.

Hypocrisy is ever with us, and we need to be alert to our tendency to deceive ourselves. Seldom are our actions and their motivations wholly pure. We cannot escape the necessity of examining the motives of our hearts. It is easier for us to examine our own motives than those of our neighbor. We cannot read another person's heart. We need, therefore, to be much quicker to judge ourselves than we are to call into question the motives of our neighbor when he or she performs a meritorious and unselfish good work. In emphasizing motivation we must avoid the error of feeling that it is only what we feel inside that counts and that external action is not necessary. First John rejects this kind of thinking quite emphatically when it says that we show love for our brother when we make specific efforts to meet his physical needs. A verbal affirmation of love falls short of the biblical definition of Christian love (1 John 3:17-18).

We can only have such motivation of love for God and for neighbor when we first realize that we ourselves are loved by God. This recognition transforms us and places within us the capacity to return that love. We are not able within ourselves to love either God or our neighbor. Consequently when we do love, we can in all honesty confess that this love is not one which we have created from within our inner beings. Rather it is a love which God has placed within our hearts so that in gratitude we love the One who has first loved us, and then, secondly, we can begin to love others who are the objects of God's love. There is no basis here for speaking of personal merit. Even our love for others is a gift from God and is an occasion to express thankfulness to him who has made the very meaning of love itself known to us.

We have been grasped by a power greater than ourselves. Consequently, the love which motivates our actions is itself a love which is greater than anything which is naturally ours. We have experienced a new birth through the Holy Spirit, and he is the channel through whom a divine love begins to transform us step by step into the new image of God which is ours through faith in Jesus Christ our Lord.

The Old and the New Ages
Christians have begun to share in the new age which through

Jesus Christ has been introduced into human history. We now experience the new age, and yet we cannot escape the reality of our involvement in the old age. We have begun to taste the fruit of the age which is to be, and this taste makes us dissatisfied with the age which now exists. Consequently, we are motivated to change what is so that it conforms more fully to the age which will one day come in power and in fullness. We live between the new and the old. We live in both, and we seek to find a way to exist as citizens of two worlds simultaneously. We belong to that which is yet to come, but we live our lives in the realm of the present world. We seek to be responsible citizens in this world. We cannot live as though the kingdom of God had already come in fullness. There remains a degree of hiddenness to the rule and sovereignty of God. It is part of our task to make that rule less hidden and less mysterious as we live under a new lordship.

We are under new management. There is no uncertainty as to where our primary loyalty belongs. We cannot serve two masters. We have one master, but we live in two realms: one in which secular values predominate and the other in which the kingdom of God and the will of God are supreme. We are on a pilgrimage which involves a march from what is to what will be. We have set our eyes upon a future day when shadows and contradictions will be gone.

THE CONSTANT CALL FOR DECISION

Ethics has its place in the tension between the old and the new ages. Since God's kingdom has not yet come in power, we keep asking ourselves how we are to exercise our Christian responsibility in this world. This question is a most complicated one since many issues and situations arise in which we can find no clear model for action in the New Testament. We are sometimes compelled to make our own judgments about what is the proper action in the light of our central motivation to serve and love God. At times there will be room for differences of opinion. Our decisions may differ from those of other Christians. This difference calls for mutual tolerance and respect.

Christian ethics cannot be viewed as timeless. We are too much tied to history and to its events to be able to plan years ahead of time what a proper Christian action would be in a hypothetical situation. We live our lives on the plain of history, and it is on this stage that we are called upon to make our decisions. The task of ethical decisions is ever with us. It is in one sense a frightful prospect, for we all ask ourselves, "Who is equal to such a responsibility?" At the same time it is a challenging and heartening one, for it tells us that God has seen fit to place this responsibility upon our shoulders. We are not being treated as minors whose decisions must largely be made for us by others. No, we are viewed as adults, as those who have reached our majority. God commits this task to us even as he committed to the church the responsibility of telling the Good News. We are co-laborers with God in the world. This gives our lives dignity and significance.

As Christians we bring into this world a foretaste of what is yet to be. We do so in fear and trembling, for we are all too much aware of the fact that our feet are feet of clay and that we very imperfectly mirror in our lives the One who is good and holy and perfect. Yet the task is ours; and in seeking to carry out the responsibility given to us, our own lives take on new meaning and purpose. We are partners with God in his work in the world.

In preparation for a recent regional Evangelistic Life-Style Retreat I prepared the following selection of principles for a Christian life-style in the twentieth century. Several of the items mentioned in this list will be discussed at greater length in subsequent chapters in this book. The table may stimulate further discussion about the meaning of a Christian life-style.

A DECALOGUE FOR A CHRISTIAN LIFE-STYLE IN THE TWENTIETH CENTURY

1. We shall acknowledge that our supreme loyalty belongs to God, and that *all* other loyalties are subordinate.

2. We shall regard all human beings as created by God and as loved by him. Consequently, we shall regard all human life as of supreme value.

3. We shall regard the earth as a God-given trust and shall strive to live in harmony not only with other human beings but also with our natural environment: the soil, the water, the air, the vegetation, animal life, and space.

4. We shall read the Bible "responsibly," recognizing the necessity of carefully interpreting its message in order to determine the Christian response it calls for in our day. This will involve, perhaps, a new appreciation of the message of the eighth-century prophets of Israel (Hosea, Isaiah, Amos, Micah), a recognition of the "newness" of Jesus' message, and an awareness on our part of the cultural conditioning reflected in scriptural commands.

5. We shall recognize that we have had our faith and practice highly shaped by tradition. What we believe comes not only from the Bible but also from the early creeds of the church and from the events of secular and religious history.

6. We shall recognize that through the Holy Spirit God continues to guide the church (John 16:12-13), and we shall stress that the primary evidence of the presence of the Spirit is not speaking in tongues nor extraordinary phenomena, but the producing of Christians who manifest maturity in Christian character and life-style.

7. We shall maintain as much concern for practice as we do for doctrine. The ethical demands of the gospel shall be as much our concern as so-called "orthodoxy" of belief.

8. We shall not regard either sex as subordinate to the other or as second-class citizens in the kingdom of God. We shall affirm our sexuality as a gift from God and seek to honor God through our full personality.

9. We shall be watchful against the threat of civil religion, for we are always in danger of so naturalizing Jesus and the Bible that any "prophetic" role the church may have in society is effectively neutralized. We shall not regard the kingdom of God as tied to any civil state or earthly government. We shall never glorify war in any manner, but shall regard it as humanity's greatest scourge. We shall regard our role in the world as reconcilers and discourage violence in the settling of domestic and international disputes.

10. We shall avoid using eschatology (that is, our beliefs regarding the Second Coming of Christ, etc.) as an escape from reality or from present responsibilities. We shall retain our hope for the future because of our confidence in the sovereignty of God and in the lordship of Jesus Christ. We shall also find in our eschatology not only a vision of what will be but also of what

ought to be. Our perception of what ought to be will serve as an incentive to personal effort to see God's will done on earth as it is in heaven. We recognize that God's ultimate kingdom will be realized only in God's time; but insofar as his will is done here and now, to that extent his kingdom is already present.

FOR FURTHER CONSIDERATION

1. Why must Christians be sensitive to life and culture around them? Do not the gospel and the Bible set up standards which can be applied without change to every age?

2. Why does Jesus play such a big part in Christian ethical decision making? Why is he given priority over other great religious leaders?

3. What is the difference between following Jesus Christ and obeying a legal ethical code?

2
Making Ethical Decisions

Christians can never make ethical decisions in a vacuum. In John we read, "If the Son makes you free, you will be free indeed" (John 8:36). This is a freedom "in Christ." It is a freedom to live according to his will, not according to ours. Luther once put it well when he said that Christians are of all people most free, but at the same time they are of all people most bound. We have been set free from the bondage to sin. At the same time we have become servants of Jesus Christ. We are not our own but have been "bought with a price" (1 Corinthians 6:20; 7:23). Paul adds, "Do not become slaves of men" (1 Corinthians 7:23). Our marching orders come from Christ, the Lord of the church.

FREE INDEED

We are not called to a life without guidance. Such a life would be a new bondage in disguise. We would then become slaves to our inner ambitions, to sensuality, to selfishness, to self-indulgence, to the desire for power or wealth or fame. The raging of these drives within us does not bring peace but turmoil. In our bondage to Christ we find perfect freedom, for now at last we can become what God intended us to be. We can fulfill our intended destiny, rather than pursuing a mirage which in the end will disappoint and destroy. In finding God we find ourselves. In serving him our own well-being is furthered. The "flesh" within us would seek to deceive us by telling us that such service is a restriction of our lives. The Spirit would remind us that every good and perfect gift comes not from self-indulgence but from a heavenly Father who spared not his own Son (Romans 8:32) because he loves us.

Freedom and Responsibility

Freedom involves responsibility. How much easier it appears to some people simply to be told in every situation what they are to do. Let others think for you. Give perfunctory obedience to external rules. In this way the mind and the heart, the inner being, are not involved in any serious decision making. People who act that way are merely functionaries. They just carry out orders, doing what superiors tell them to do. Is this the kind of obedience God demands of those who have become his children through regeneration? As members of God's new age which is dawning, we are asked for a response which involves the whole person. Mechanical observance of rules is not what the New Testament means when it talks about Christian discipleship.

Freedom can be a joy if exercised to the glory of God. It can be a heavy burden if we are torn by conflicting loyalties, if we have not determined within ourselves who is the real master of our lives. The result can be a constant and devastating inner conflict. We will always be torn between the options before us. To live with the responsibility of freedom under such circumstances is to live in confusion, restlessness, and anxiety. We must first resolve the issue of lordship, namely, "Who is my master?" Until this has been settled, we can find no peace. Only then can we become what God intended us to be. In finding him, we find ourselves.

Any set of rules, any legal code, any exhaustive list of "dos" and "don'ts" robs the Christian of his or her freedom. Such a legal view of life takes away from us mature ethical response. True freedom exists where our actions emerge from conscious decision and not from a reflex response. We are sons and daughters of God, not unthinking, programmed machines.

Making ethical decisions may often become more difficult rather than easier the more we reflect on the implications involved in our actions. Christian ethics does not involve the formation or memorizing of an objective code which we then seek carefully to follow. There is no code which can address all circumstances. Life is too full of variety and newness to allow for such a wooden application of Christian principles to daily experiences. As Christians we bear the privilege and the responsibility of Christian freedom.

We are called upon to exercise personal judgment every time ethical decisions confront us. This can be a burden, especially if the issue before us is complex and one where we may even conclude that no action we can take will completely fulfill the ideals of the Christian life-style. The contamination of the world and its values so permeates the sphere in which we live that few decisions we make will be pure and ethically unmixed. We are compelled to choose between options which in some cases involve a degree of accommodation or compromise no matter what we do. Awareness of this ambiguity can lead to despair, but it should not. In such instances we remind ourselves again of the grace of God and act with a humble prayer for the continued forgiveness of God as we participate in the affairs of "the world" of which we are a part. We are reminded that we can never fully escape its contamination until the "age to come."

Because of the ever-changing circumstances of life, ethical decisions can never be determined with finality prior to the challenge of the moment. They cannot be prefabricated and then put into place without modification. To a high degree, ethical decisions which are responsible decisions involve "custom" thinking. They need to be "tailor-made" to fit the peculiar and distinctive dimensions of each ethical demand made upon us.

Three Approaches to Christian Ethics

A person can conceivably have a view of ethics which regards all possible situations as covered by some ethical rule. Such a legalistic approach to ethics we can call *code morality*.[1] For every problem there is a fixed answer. There are difficulties with this view of ethics. Codes reflect historical situations, and they must be interpreted in the light of the circumstances which existed when they emerged. We must take such historical factors into consideration when we seek to apply past codes to present situations. In other words, we must use them responsibly. Another caution that needs to be expressed is that obeying a set of laws may result in an impersonal legalism. The Christian needs to remember that responsible ethical decisions emerge not from adherence to a legal code but from a new personal relationship which we have with God through Jesus Christ. Another error to avoid is that of giving the impression that through obedience to a set of rules we are justified by human effort, that is, by good works. The gospel affirms that it is only by the grace of God revealed in Jesus Christ and through faith that we can be justified before God. Past codes are better used as guides for ethical behavior than as fixed rules which are always to be obeyed without question.

A second approach to ethics may be called *principle morality*. Here the stress is on general moral principles which have universal application. These principles are not limited to specific people, places, or times. An example of such a moral principle would be the command that we are to love our neighbor. This approach avoids the legalism found when codes are stressed, but it puts a considerable burden on us as individuals. We know that we are supposed to love, but how are we to express that love in a given situation? This concern remains something which each one of us needs to decide for oneself.

Codes and principles are both needed because they give us a place to begin. We have to add to them, however, reflection on their meaning in the particular situations in which we are called upon to make decisions. The concern to relate ethical laws and principles to specific situations has given rise to what may be called a third approach to ethics, namely, *situational ethics*. This emphasis has also been called "contextual or relational ethics." In this approach it is maintained that each situation we face is in some ways unique. As mature Christian people we need to face every ethical situation in the light of all the circumstances involved.

An example may help to illustrate what we have just said. A friend of our family hid her son during the occupation of Holland in the Second World War. When authorities came to the door searching for young men, she had to ask herself, "Shall I tell them the truth that I have a son hiding in the house or shall I not?" She had to weigh the alternatives. Should she vote for "truth" or for "freedom and life"? She could see no way of violating an ethical principle whichever way she decided. She chose "life" over against simply telling the truth to persons who were acting in violation of what she considered to be the law and will of God. Can we sit in judgment on her decision? When such conflict situations arise, we all need to judge what is the highest good in the light of our knowledge of the will of God and in consideration of the specific circumstances which we are then facing.

Mature Christian decisions will involve a concern for all three of the elements we have discussed: codes, principles, and situations. Our stress will not be on blind obedience to an external code. Our primary concern will be to consider what best expresses the will of God in each and every circumstance in which we find ourselves. We are sons and daughters of God, and as such we are called upon to make our ethical decisions in the light of the best knowledge available to us.

The Motivating Power of Love

The primary motivation behind Christian decisions must be love. Love cannot be ordered. It must exist within us if it is to be the moving force of our lives. Love itself is a gift from God. Paul writes, "God's love has been poured into our hearts through the Holy Spirit which has been given to us" (Romans 5:5). Because we love God, our Christian service is not a burden, but a privilege. We are dealing here with something deeper and finer than obedience to legal demands made upon us from without. We serve and obey God from overflowing and grateful hearts.

Ethics does not show us what we *must* do, but what in thankfulness we *may* do. Remember the inscription on a sculpture at a boys' school in the Midwest. An older boy is shown carrying a younger boy on his back. In reply to the question "Isn't he heavy?" the older one says, "He's not heavy. He's my brother." The service of love is no burden; it is the spontaneous response of the heart.

We need to be freed for love. As long as self-love, love of things, love of personal recognition, and love of power sway our lives, we are not free, but bound. When we have been set free from all these fetters, we can be free indeed—free to love God and free to serve our neighbor.

THE KINGDOM OF GOD VERSUS THE WORLD

Ethics is ultimately determined not by our relationship to the world, but by our relationship to God. There exists an ultimate conflict between the values represented by the world and the ideals of the kingdom of God. The more sensitive we become to the distinctive demands of the kingdom of God, the more we also become aware of the areas of conflict with the world. As this awareness increases, we will sense the need to implement in our daily lives a life-style which can be lived realistically in the world. Modern society is not conducive to Christ's values. Indifference at best, open hostility at worst, is the world's response to such standards. As followers of the Christ, however, we are determined to affirm our loyalty to him and not to the world's alien system.

No easy truce can be reached between these two perspectives. At times there may be areas of mutual interest, and in these areas cooperation is possible. Humanitarian concerns, for example, do not usually reflect an area in which church and society at large would disagree. Sometimes action in the world will involve some degree of compromise. We are, after all, in the world even if we are not "of the world" (John 17:16). We must, therefore, develop a realistic outlook on what is possible in a world in which God's values are at the edge of society's thinking, if not completely excluded.

If we allow the world to determine our ethics, then we are living as though we belonged to the world. We belong instead to God. To conform to the world's point of view is to lose any witness to the world. We can then have no message for our contemporaries. Before becoming believers in Christ the lives many of us lived were determined by "worldly" standards (see Ephesians 2:1-2). The challenge which comes to us is to live a new life-style. Paul writes, "Do not be conformed to this world but be transformed by the renewal of your mind, that you may prove what is the will of God, what is good and acceptable and perfect" (Romans 12:2). Full transformation does not occur overnight. The progressive idea contained in the words actually used by Paul is captured admirably in Charles B. Williams's translation of this verse. His rendering is as follows:

> Stop living in accordance with the customs of this world, but by the new ideals that mould your minds continue to transform yourselves, so as to find and follow God's will; that is, what is good, well-pleasing to Him, and perfect.

When we live by the will of God, we can be assured that the world will notice that we do not conform to the accepted pattern. This will cause surprise (1 Peter 4:4) and perhaps hostility (John 15:18-19; 17:14). Friction is inevitable. Jesus warned his disciples, "Woe to you, when all men speak well of you, for so their fathers did to the false prophets" (Luke 6:26).

We cannot escape involvement in the world. Our presence in the world is compared by Jesus to "sheep in the midst of wolves" (Matthew 10:16). We cannot ignore the world. We live in the world; we minister in the world. Not only that, but to a degree the world lives in us. This awareness should lead to a considerable degree of humility. We cannot simply stand in judgment on the world and on our neighbor. We are all contaminated by the alien values represented by the world. It is only by the grace of God that we have been delivered from the world's control. The battle continues for as long as we live. Consequently the matter of decision making is ever with us. Deciding for Christ and the life-style of the "new age" is a daily and even hourly responsibility.

God has not rejected or repudiated the world, despite its sin and fallenness (John 3:16). He has rescued us from it and is not desirous that "any should perish" (2 Peter 3:9). Our task in the world is to be instruments of God's peace so that the Good News may reach others whose lives are now ruled by sin and not by God (Matthew 28:19-20).

Conflict Situations

In the real world in which we live ethical decisions are often not matters of choosing between black and white options. There are times when it seems that, no matter what decision we make, we are violating some biblical principle. This causes pangs of conscience, but we cannot become immobilized so that we withdraw from the responsibility before us. There are times when we must make decisions and we have to choose between shades of gray. Such a realistic look at ethics might be called the ethics of compromise. We cannot water down the Christian imperative, but we have to be realistic in seeking to apply the imperative in given situations. We are, therefore, involved in what could be termed "situational" ethics.

There are two extremes which we need to avoid. As we find the need for this kind of compromise, we need to stay clear of an attitude of total despair, feeling that Christian ethics do not apply in the real world of everyday decision making. The other extreme is to decide that there are really two compartments to life: the inner and personal life of faith to which Christian ethics applies, and the outer and social world in which we have our daily tasks in which some alternative, practical, worldly code of behavior becomes the standard of reference in making decisions. When this latter view takes over, we have become callous and indifferent to Christian values. We live schizophrenic lives. We have a personal life of faith but a public life shaped by the value system of the world of business and industry. This separation may result in a pseudo sense of security where we live without pangs of conscience, but it is in reality an escape from wrestling with the meaning of Christian discipleship in every area of life. Jesus is the Lord of all life. We cannot confine his lordship to the limited sphere of the church, the family, or the inner personal lives of believers.

To steer a course through this troubled sea is far from a simple task. Jesus said, "Render therefore to Caesar the things that are Caesar's, and to God the things that are God's" (Matthew 22:21). This sets before us the dilemma we face, but it does not give any clear indication where the line between the two can be drawn, nor does it indicate what our action is to be when the two realms are in open conflict with one another. Presumably when the latter is the case, the supreme loyalty which we owe to God overrules the loyalty which we owe to the state. But what happens when the state is partly right and partly wrong? What do we do in such a situation? It is this borderline ethical problem which causes us the greatest anguish and difficulty. It is here that we need guidance and help.

The Possibility of Alternative Choices

There is one delusion which can easily overtake us and which we need to avoid. In many areas of ethical conflict reasonable persons may differ in their opinions as to what is the preferred action which should be taken. When this happens, we should not assume that one approach is inevitably more ethically defensible or more correct than another. We need to remember that in most borderline situations there is more than one possible course of action which could be defended as the best one to take at a given moment. It is possible that all choices involve a degree of compromise. There may be no basis whatever for saying that action "a" is clearly more supportable that actions "b" or "c." We each must face the challenge of ethical decision making before God. When we have come to our decision, we do so with at least the inner assurance that we have sought in the decision to act responsibly to our understanding of Christian ethics. Other sincere Christians may have come to different decisions. They, too, can leave their decision in the hands of God and not be forever troubled by the feeling that their decision may have been in error. We cannot remain forever undecided. We seek to act in good conscience, and we can then leave the matter with God.

The Need for Continued Forgiveness

No matter what our decisions may be in these matters of conflict, we make them with a deep awareness of our involvement in "the world." The world remains a place of sin and disobedience. Because we are in the world and in some measure still a part of the world, our own decisions will be tainted by sin. Consequently, we can only plead the merits of Christ for our forgiveness. We choose the best alternative before us, and yet we sometimes cannot avoid violating our understanding of some aspect of the Christian imperative. The assurance of the forgiveness of God in such a conflicting situation can give us peace of mind. We recognize that the fallen world of which we are a part sometimes involves us in sin where we have no choice. We cannot be self-righteous for we are sinners, but neither do we allow ourselves to be crushed by pangs of conscience. A Christian sensitivity helps us to face such conflict situations with some degree of objectivity and realism. Without God's forgiveness we simply cannot function in the real world of human society.

THE QUANTITATIVE NATURE OF ETHICAL DECISIONS

Statements of doctrine are dogmatic. Things are thus and so and not otherwise. There is a qualitative distinction maintained between truth and error, between orthodoxy and heresy. Matters are held to be more or less black and white. This distinct line between alternatives does not always exist in the area of Christian ethics. Here we face a multitude of alternatives, many of which share aspects of truth and elements of error. Pure ethical decisions are rare. Even when we act in a commendable way, we would probably have to acknowledge that the motives behind our actions are often mixed. Love of God and love of neighbor may play a part, but self-interest has a way of weaving itself into most of our decisions and actions. The result is that when we leave "dogmatics" (or doctrine) and come to "ethics," we leave the qualitative and become involved in what Helmut Thielicke has aptly termed the "quantitative." The insight which he expresses seems especially helpful at this point. He writes:

> . . . when ethics is dealing with concrete decisions, it always moves in the sphere of the quantitative, of what is more or less right. It would be a false abstraction, an illegitimate ignoring of the conflict situation, to think that we are always faced by clear-cut alternatives, or, in view of our total sinfulness, to cultivate ethical indifference by supposing that all acts come under the same condemnation. . . . One sin, then, is not like another.[2]

Earlier in his book he made the observation,

> . . . this aeon [is a] zone of relativities. . . .
> When it comes to the question of concretely fulfilling the demands of the Sermon on the Mount we shall always have to enter into a consideration of various degrees. . . .[3]

Jesus, himself, approached the requirements of the law in much the same way. Healing an individual on the sabbath was a higher demand than the law's demanding that people refrain from labor on that day. Jesus cited the example of David who ate the bread of the Presence from the temple and gave his men the same bread to eat when again according to the law only the priests were to eat this bread (Matthew 12:3-4). Jesus gave this example after his disciples were accused of laboring on the sabbath when they ate grains of wheat as they walked through a grain field on the sabbath day. Jesus summed it up by saying that "mercy," not "sacrifice," is the higher principle by which we are to live (Matthew 12:7).

Facing Criticism

There will always be those who will criticize our actions. This is unavoidable. We will need to be persuaded in our own minds concerning the rightness of our actions and leave the rest with God. God is our judge, not our fellow human beings. Paul reminds us of this principle when he writes, "Who are you to pass judgment on the servant of another? It is before his own master that he stands or falls. And he will be upheld, for the Master is able to make him stand" (Romans 14:4).

When Christians differ on a proper course of action, a side benefit may emerge. The minority decision may serve to remind the other Christians that there is more than one Christian view which can be held with full integrity. This can have two very significant results. First of all, it can make all of us more tolerant of others. It can lead us to acknowledge the possibility of these alternatives and make us ready to defend the right of our fellow Christians to hold these views. Secondly, the minority report can act as a stimulus to keep issues open for further consideration and discussion. Difference of views among Christians need not be regretted. Such difference should lead to humility. We don't have all the answers. The existence of differences should also keep us from complacency, the feeling that we have solved the issue at hand. Perhaps the minority point of view will contain some insight into Christian discipleship which the majority has overlooked. Through dialogue there can be mutual enlightenment. The end result may be a more satisfactory application of Christian values and ideals to the situation at hand.

The views of Mahatma Gandhi, for example, presented one alternative to the use of force to achieve one's ethical ends. Some regarded his views as impractical in the modern world. Yet India's independence from England was achieved without major bloodshed or widespread damage to property. This is not to say that Gandhi's approach will always work, but we must acknowledge that it is a defensible alternative to those who advocate the use of violence. Gandhi acknowledged that his views were influenced by the Sermon on the Mount as well as the writings of Leo Tolstoy and the Indian Scriptures known as the Bhagavad Gita, an important expression of Hinduism. While Gandhi did not profess to be a Christian, his views incorporated insights which came from the teachings of Jesus.

The Cost of Decisions

Some decisions we make for Christ may well be unpopular, either with other Christians or with "the world." In that case we may be called upon to bear the cross of ridicule, persecution, and even death. This may be the road of discipleship for some Christians. Steadfast witness to the truth as we see it honors the God we serve and presents in a clear way the challenge of Christian discipleship to the world. The gospel and the cause of Christ are often advanced by men and women who take their discipleship seriously enough to be willing to stand up for the ideals they believe in and to be vocal concerning their faith. Where and how we can each make our contribution to the ongoing work of God needs to be discovered by each one of us in the particular place in which God and circumstances have put us.

We are all individuals before God. No two paths of discipleship may be identical. Each of the disciples of Jesus had his own strengths and limitations. So it will be with us. The cross and our loyalty to Jesus Christ are the factors which unite us. We build on this foundation, and we build together. Over and above all of our efforts there is the assurance of the sovereignty of God. God's kingdom will ultimately prevail not because of the activity of men and women, but because of the grace, power, and faithfulness of our heavenly Father. It is our privilege to be called by him into personal faith and into obedient service in his name in the world.

FOR FURTHER CONSIDERATION

1. Christians are free. What limits or guides that freedom?

2. With respect to Christian freedom what is the difference between deciding something *for ourselves* and deciding *on our own,* that is, independently? What part should the Christian community have in shaping our individual decisions?

3. What are some of the social pressures that influence the values and behavior of both young people and adults? Would it be desirable to be completely free from all social pressures? Why or why not?

3
A Code to Obey or a Life to Live?

If we are called to follow Christ in faithful service, what directions do we have? Many find help in the Sermon on the Mount. Others turn to the law or conscience for guidance. The biblical description of the person as created in the image of God or as a steward of creation is also helpful. But all of these attempts to define codes of conduct lead to frustration or despair unless we have committed ourselves to life in Christ.

THE SERMON ON THE MOUNT

The Sermon on the Mount has quite appropriately been called "A Pattern for Life."[1] In Matthew we have this sermon presented in chapters 5 through 7. Most scholars regard these chapters as a summary of the ethical teachings of Jesus which for instructional purposes have been gathered together and presented in one place in Matthew's Gospel. The things taught here were probably spoken many times by Jesus. As the message of Jesus was repeated orally in the years between his ascension and the writing of the gospels, some thirty to fifty years later, his ethical teachings

37

were collected and presented here in Matthew 5 to 7 as a unit.

The Kingdom of God

The central theme of the Sermon on the Mount is the kingdom of God. By this term Jesus referred to the rule, the reign, or the sovereignty of God. Early Christians regarded this world as subject to two kingdoms—the kingdom of God and the kingdom of darkness. Followers of Jesus believed that in a new and powerful way the rule of God came into history in the person of Jesus Christ. Those who confessed his lordship and became his disciples acknowledged that God was working in a unique way in Jesus Christ and that in his life the power of God for good and for salvation had been brought to humanity. The resurrection of Jesus Christ from the dead was God's confirming sign that this was indeed true. Subsequently the gift to the church of the Holy Spirit, who was identified as the Spirit of Christ, the one who continued Christ's work on earth, was further proof that God was indeed acting in and through Jesus of Nazareth for the redemption of the world.

In acknowledging Jesus as Lord, his followers became subjects of the kingdom of God. This did not mean that the kingdom of darkness did not continue to be a temptation for them or a cause of continual opposition. They had, however, cast their lot with God over against evil and were willing to endure whatever hardships this involved. There were times of failure, admittedly, but there followed repentance and restoration as they once again took up their cross and followed Christ and his teachings.

To follow Jesus does not mean to follow a strict code in some legalistic fashion. It means rather to have a new loyalty. This changed loyalty gives altered perspectives and with it new values and purposes. The goals of the kingdom stand in sharp contrast to the ideals of the world. Since the kingdom and the world represent opposite values, a situation of real or potential conflict is always present between God's kingdom and the kingdom of darkness.

In speaking of these two kingdoms, we must be careful to avoid the error of thinking that they are external to each one of us. Our own lives are small reflections of both the kingdom of God and the kingdom of darkness. Although we have transferred our loyalty to

Jesus Christ, we realize that the standards admired and worshiped by the world have an echo within our own hearts. The values which are hostile to the will of God reside not only in the external world but also within ourselves. This is why temptation is always before us. We are drawn by the glitter of the world because the world lives in us. The battle of discipleship is a lifelong struggle and even a daily one. We are to "put to death" that which is unrighteous in us, in order that God's full work in our lives may be accomplished (Romans 8:13). The presence of God's Spirit within us as our Helper is the guarantee that we can overcome the power of the evil one.

Faith as Personal Commitment

At the heart of discipleship is faith. Faith means a personal commitment to God and, as understood from the perspective of the New Testament, a personal commitment to Jesus Christ as Lord. Discipleship is not fulfilled by obedience or good works. Good works follow a personal commitment to Jesus Christ as Lord. We join together faith in God and faith in Jesus of Nazareth because Jesus came to reveal the Father. God was in Christ reconciling the world to himself.

"Do Not Be Anxious"

One of the results of faith is the assurance that we have been accepted by the Father and that we are loved by him. Furthermore there is the conviction that God is sovereign in this universe and that all of history is under his control. While evil may appear to flourish, the days of darkness are numbered. We are marching toward the dawn, and we have the inner assurance that we are the children of light.

Such assurance is a cure for anxiety. This is the real meaning of the words found in Matthew 6:34, which in the King James Version reads as follows: "Take therefore no thought for the morrow: for the morrow shall take thought for the things of itself" (Matthew 6:34). When we hear these words, we instinctively wonder if this is good counsel. Is Jesus urging his followers to be thoughtless, to be careless and irresponsible about the future? We certainly do not normally regard thoughtlessness as praiseworthy. It is generally considered a weakness of character rather than a virtue. In this verse we face an interpretation problem. The passage is rendered much more precisely in *The New English Bible* where we read, "So do not be anxious about tomorrow; tomorrow will look after itself."

This passage speaks not of irresponsibility but of anxiety. Anxiety is a painful uneasiness of mind regarding some feared future event which may bring to us pain, sorrow, or loss. That Jesus was not suggesting a careless attitude toward the future is clear from many other statements he made. On one occasion he pointed out the foolishness of a person who would begin building a watchtower without first considering whether or not he had enough material on hand to complete the project. Similarly he said it would be foolhardy for a king who had ten thousand soldiers at his command to launch an attack against another king who could put twenty thousand men in the field.

Regarding the future few of us are totally thoughtless. Most of us carry life insurance, accident insurance, fire insurance, and unemployment insurance, and we are active members of Social Security and perhaps of private pension plans. The government also provides Medicare, veterans' disability pensions, old-age pensions, and various welfare programs. We recognize the value of making a will in order to arrange for a proper disposition of our property at our death. All of these plans are needed and helpful in modern society. A close-knit group like the Amish can provide adequately for themselves. The exception, however, proves the rule that such a pattern of living is foolhardy for the majority of us rather than a wise life-style to adopt.

In the verse before us Jesus is talking about "anxiety" and not about careful planning for emergencies. We are all open to various kinds of anxiety. Young people worry about popularity. Adults worry about job security and job advancement. We are all concerned about health, possible bereavement, loneliness, and a score of other matters that trouble us from time to time. What counsel does Jesus give us that would support his command, "Do not be anxious"? What realities must be true for us if we are to take seriously this counsel and live day by day without undue anxiety and worry? Are there some foundational pillars upon which to build as we seek to lead creative and positive Christian lives?

The first principle which seems to emerge in all of Jesus' teachings is that it is important that we establish *proper priorities* in our lives. What do we put first in our lives? Jesus said, "Where your treasure is, there will your heart be also" (Matthew 6:21). A person's scale of values determines the direction of that person's life. No personal interest or value must become so central in our thinking that it displaces our primary loyalty to God himself. Personal possessions can easily take the place of God; and when they do, we do not possess them; they possess us. An ancient philosopher once said, "Wealth is the slave of a wise man, the master of a fool." Along a similar vein Martin Luther is reported to have said, "To have money and property is not sin, only you must not let it be your master, but you must be its master."

To state this principle positively, we can quote the words of Jesus when he said, "But seek first his kingdom and his righteousness, and all these things shall be yours as well" (Matthew 6:33). We all have our priorities whether or not we have given much thought to them or have ever tried to list them. By looking objectively at that to which we devote our time and on which we spend our energy and money, we can soon have a fairly clear picture of what we regard as of most importance in our lives.

A second principle which emerges from the New Testament is that we are to *live responsibly*. Work is honored in Scripture, not slothfulness or idleness. The Jewish rabbis had a saying, "He who does not teach his son a trade teaches him to steal." Even rabbis were taught a trade, and they were not ashamed to work with their hands. We recall that Paul made tents and in this way supported himself in his missionary travels.

Paul rebuked some Christians at Thessalonica who had given up their employment and were spending their time in idleness. His words were short and clear about them. He said, "Now such persons we command and exhort in the Lord Jesus Christ to do their work in quietness and to earn their own living" (2 Thessalonians 3:12). He sharply scolds their behavior with the words, "If any one will not work, let him not eat" (2 Thessalonians 3:10).

A third cure for anxiety lies in a steadfast *trust* in God. We are to have faith in a loving heavenly Father who knows and cares. This is good news. God loves us. God cares about us. God is with us in every crisis of our lives. We need to trust him. Remember the words of the Lord Jesus who said, "Your heavenly Father knows that you need them all" (Matthew 6:32). Jesus supports this exhortation with an illustration of God's hand in nature:

> But if God so clothes the grass of the field, which today is alive and tomorrow is thrown into the oven, will he not much more clothe you, O men of little faith? Therefore do not be anxious, saying, "What shall we eat?" or "What shall we drink?" or "What shall we wear?" (Matthew 6:30-31).

What Jesus is urging is responsible living supported by faith. We are to do what we can, and then we may leave the rest in the hands of a merciful and loving heavenly Father. A motto placed over the entrance of an inn in England read as follows:

Fear knocked at the door. Faith answered. There was no one there.

Faith casts out fear. In 1 Peter 5:7 we are exhorted with these words, "Cast all your anxieties on him, for he cares about you." Again in Philippians 4:6-7 we read:

> Have no anxiety about anything, but in everything by prayer and supplication with thanksgiving let your requests be made known to God. And the peace of God, which passes all understanding, will keep your hearts and your minds in Christ Jesus.

In the light of promises such as these we can understand more readily the exhortation found in the Sermon on the Mount when Jesus says, "So do not be anxious about tomorrow; tomorrow will look after itself" (Matthew 6:34, *The New English Bible*).

Law and Grace

Some persons have misread the Sermon on the Mount and take it to be a new law patterned after or improving upon the law of Moses. This it is not. It is not presented as a legal code. It is not a list of "Dos" and "Don'ts" by which we either earn merit or feel guilty. Rather it sets forth the kind of life that honors God and demonstrates the presence of the kingdom (and of the King) in our lives. It is a pattern for life, not a binding code. The law was an external code introduced because of humanity's fall and sinfulness. The Sermon on the Mount speaks primarily to those who have become partakers of a new creation. They have become sharers in the new age which entered the world with the coming of Jesus Christ. As members of that new age their lives have been transformed, and the evidence of the transformation which has already taken place is the new life-style which they display.

PERSONAL COMMITMENT TO CHRIST

Christian ethics can never be reduced to a code, whether it be the Sermon on the Mount, or the teachings of Paul, or any document subsequently prepared by the church in the following centuries. Christian life remains forever primarily a relationship to God and to Jesus Christ. Christianity centers in personal commitment. Out of that personal commitment obedience follows. What obedience means in a given situation can seldom be determined ahead of time abstractly. Christian discipleship is a matter which needs to be hammered out on the anvil of life's experiences. Each of us must ask, "What at this moment is the way of discipleship for me?" Just to follow a preconceived plan which I have inherited is not to make mature decisions for God. It is to follow a legalistic code in which my heart may be far removed from genuine submission to the will of a sovereign and loving heavenly Father. God treats us as maturing followers, not as slaves who have no choice but to carry out prescribed procedures.

The Function of the Law

Why then the law at all? This question is hardly a new one. Paul anticipated just such a response in Romans when he wrote: "What shall we say then? Are we to continue in sin that grace may abound? By no means! How can we who died to sin still live in it?" (Romans 6:1-2). Paul regards the law as good and as a gift of God. It can serve as a guide, but not as a code. Motivations are all important. God looks on the heart, not on external action alone. The lustful thought and the adulterous act both need to be brought under our new loyalty to God, as must both hatred and murder.

The law reminds us of how imperfectly we obey God. We are humbled by its absolute demands. It therefore serves to drive us again and again to God for forgiveness. It is only by his grace and mercy that we can stand before him. Our works merit no acceptance with a holy and righteous God. We are now and ever shall be sinners in need of divine forgiveness.

This does not mean that the law is an enemy. It serves to remind us of the rocks and pitfalls at the side of the road: "Be careful." "Soft shoulder." "Danger." "Drive slowly." Thielicke describes the role of the law in a colorful manner:

> ... the Law is a kind of sheep dog whose purpose is to recall the members of the flock to the path of the shepherd. Now it is the shepherd who does the leading, not the dog. It is not the dog but the shepherd who is the center and focal point of the flock, the one to whom the sheep know themselves to be related.[2]

In Christ we have a higher standard than the law, but the law is useful to give concrete images to the high ideals of love for God and love for neighbor. The law helps to teach us the will of God. It is one resource among others which helps us to understand God's will for humanity. It reminds us that discipleship means obedience. The law does not now exist to condemn us, for we have been delivered from its condemnation by the grace of God. It continues rather to set before us a guideline by which to live. In looking at that standard, however, we cannot act as if Jesus had never come. In his teachings on the inner motivation we see that an external code is not enough. The law can remain as a teacher, but never as a taskmaster.

Conscience

Paul speaks at times in his letters regarding conscience and of the relationship of conscience to the life-styles by which we live (see 1 Corinthians 10:28-29). Through conscience we can have a sense of guilt or a sense that what we are doing is right. This inner judgment on our actions can never, however, replace the objective standard of the Scriptures and must be subject to what in Scripture has been revealed concerning the will of God. The pangs of an accusing conscience can be silenced by an acceptance in faith of the Good News of the gospel which tells us that in Jesus Christ we are forgiven and accepted. We need to go again and again to this great news so that we can live as free persons, free to do the will of God from the heart. Our freedom is not one of license, that is, the freedom to live without restraint. Rather it is the freedom to be able to serve God. As Christians we are set free from the shackles of sin which bind us and control our lives. Only in his father's house does the prodigal son really find the freedom to fulfill his potential, to become what destiny prepared him to be. Away from the father's house he finds not freedom but the tyranny of many masters—ambition, pride, money, inner drives, and so forth. In God's bondage we find perfect freedom. We serve God not because we must but because we may, because through his Spirit he makes it possible for us to walk tall.

Conscience, once it has been submitted to the will of God, can become for us an inner voice calling us back again and again to the ways of God. It can remind us of the need to put to death those things in our lives which are alien to the will of God, and it can challenge us afresh with the true meaning of discipleship. It holds before us constantly the meaning of the gospel, both as God's "gift" and as his "task."

The Image of God

Men and women have been created in the image of God (Genesis 1:26-27). This tells us not only who we are but also what we are to become. We are God's representatives on the earth. As such, a certain quality of life is expected of us. In the New Testament Jesus is spoken of as the image of God (Colossians 1:15). This is altogether appropriate because he is the only person who ever lived who fully revealed the Father. All others are very imperfect representatives of the Creator.

Paul urges the Corinthian believers to be imitators of him as he is of Christ (1 Corinthians 11:1). This is not a boast but implies that they should follow his example to the extent that they see the lifestyle of Jesus Christ reproduced in him. It is not wrong to speak of imitating Christ provided we realize that there will always remain both a quantitative and a qualitative difference between Jesus and the rest of humankind. His obedience was total; ours is always partial. Qualitatively he bore a unique relationship with the

Father, one which is not now, nor ever will be, ours. He was the Son of God who was incarnate in the world in order to reveal the Father and to provide redemption for humanity.

Paul reminds the Christians at Colossae that they have "put on the new nature, which is being renewed in knowledge after the image of its creator" (Colossians 3:10). His intent is to remind them that he expects a new life-style from them. Their lives should reflect their new nature. There is always in the Bible a tension between what is true in the plan and eyes of God and what is true in human experience. It is the tension between the "indicative" and the "imperative." What God has affirmed to be the case we are urged to appropriate and make genuinely ours by obedient and faithful discipleship.

The image of God is both a gift and a task. It is what God has given to us, and at the same time it is an ideal which is held up before our eyes as a goal for which we are to strive with full earnestness. God has made us so that we may have fellowship with him. We, however, need to fulfill that potential by walking in a manner pleasing to him (1 John 1:3, 6-7).

Fellowship is not something which is automatic. It must be cultivated and maintained. This is our responsibility. God seeks fellowship with us and is always available to us when we call upon him. Only rebellion and sin can become barriers between us and God and make fellowship impossible. Ultimately the image of God is something which God gives to us and is not ours by nature. We reflect that image only to the extent that we maintain a relationship of obedience and fellowship with the Creator. Only then can we truly be his representatives in the world, rule over the created order as God's custodians, and walk in righteousness as redeemed men and women, growing toward maturity in Christian character and life-style.

According to the New Testament, Jesus Christ is the one who in a unique way is "the image of the invisible God" (Colossians 1:15; 2 Corinthians 4:4). The New Testament speaks of Christians as bearing this image not because they, like Adam, were made in God's image, but because their lives are submitted in obedience to Jesus Christ as Lord. We bear God's image, in other words, only to the extent that we let Christ rule our lives. In fact God has predestined believers to be "conformed to the image of his Son" (Romans 8:29). To some degree this is something which becomes ours as we grow in grace and Christian maturity. In another sense it remains a future hope, one which will be fully ours only at the time of the resurrection. It is only then that we shall fully bear the "image of the man of heaven" (1 Corinthians 15:49).

The image of God in our lives has to do with our relationship to Christ. The closer we walk with him, the more the image will become a reality for us. The farther we walk from him, the less will his image be visible. Any light which we shed in this world is ultimately a reflected light. It is Christ who is the light of the world. When we walk with him in fellowship, then it can be said of us, "You are the light of the world" (Matthew 5:14).

Stewards of the Earth's Resources

Immediately after speaking of man and woman as created in the image of God, the writer of Genesis affirms that God said, ". . . let them have dominion over the fish of the sea, and over the birds of the air, and over the cattle, and over all the earth, and over every creeping thing that creeps upon the earth" (Genesis 1:26). As in the case of animal life, the plants and the trees were also entrusted to humanity to be for us a source of food (Genesis 1:29). The rule of men and women over the earth was to be a responsible one. They were to be keepers of the animals, caretakers of the land, and gardeners for the fruits and vegetables of the earth. The animals and the plant life were gifts from God for our proper use. They were a trust and a responsibility. The gift was not for one generation only but for as long as humans lived upon the earth.

Today we see misuse of these resources. We see a raping of the earth. We see chemical destruction of fields and forests. In the past the forests have been carelessly cut down without adequate provision for new growth of timber. Many species of animals and birds are becoming extinct. Some of our lakes have been so filled with the debris of industry that they can no longer sustain life. Our rivers are full of sewage, and the oceans are beginning to reduce the plant and fish life within them. Our air is impure; and as more pollutants enter it year by year, it will grow worse.

We are failing in our stewardship of the natural resources which

God has entrusted to us. A proper theology of creation would remind us that we are God's representatives on earth. This implies a proper use and preservation of the rich heritage which the earth represents. We have seen the barrenness of the moon. The beauty of the earth stands out all the more sharply in contrast to the moon's wastelands. We owe it to God, to ourselves, and to future generations to take care of God's good earth. Taking care of the environment is not only a sensible thing to do, but it also can be viewed as a valid aspect of Christian discipleship. Our faith has implications for the full range of human life and experience.

FOR FURTHER CONSIDERATION

1. Do you agree that the church and the world overlap? In what ways is this so?

2. What forms our consciences? Can they be nurtured to work for us? If so, how?

3. Why has the problem of ecology, or the use of natural resources, only become a widespread concern to people in recent years? How do you relate your Christian faith to a responsible use of the air, water, and land around us?

4
Christian Discipleship

To be a follower of Jesus is to be a disciple. As we recall the first disciples of Jesus, we realize that, though sharing a common calling, each one was called to make a unique contribution. Paul further points out that each one who would be a disciple is called to grow into maturity as God works within.

THE FIRST DISCIPLES OF JESUS

It was evening. The sun had set. As Jesus and his disciples entered the upper room, their entrance caused the clay oil lamps to flicker, and the dancing flames cast giant shadows around the room. The men filed in quietly and took their places at the low table. In imagination, let us join the disciples as they converse quietly together. A glance at their hands and faces reveals that these bronzed men were men of the outdoors. Their rough hands tell of the physical labor by which most of them were accustomed to pursue their livelihoods.

They were certainly a mixed company. First, there was Peter, the natural spokesman for the group, a strong impulsive man who readily spoke his mind and to whom the others gave respect and looked for leadership. His brother, Andrew, was quieter in his ways but also eager and decisive. He was not afraid to share what he discovered to be true. He was Jesus' first disciple, and it was he who brought Peter to Jesus and introduced him, saying, "We have found the Christ." These two brothers, like their partners in the fishing industry, James and John, were not irreligious men. They were disciples of John the Baptist before they were disciples of Jesus. This indicates that they were men who were looking for the kingdom of righteousness promised by the prophets. In all probability, each sabbath found the two pairs of brothers in attendance at the synagogue in Capernaum, which was located just a few hundred yards from the shoreline where the waves of the lake beat their incessant rhythm on the rocks which outlined the harbor.

One day, early in the morning, while mending their nets, Jesus came to them and challenged them to follow him. This was not their first meeting. They had met him before when they were with John the Baptist. The call to discipleship may well have been anticipated. In any case, without hesitation, they left their nets and for the next three years became constant companions of Jesus as he proclaimed the gospel of God throughout Galilee, Samaria, and Judea.

As we return in imagination to the upper room, we find sitting near Peter and Andrew the two brothers, James and John. James tended to be quiet and thoughtful, but he was a dependable and devout disciple. Despite his quiet ways, there was also an aggressiveness in him. He and his brother, John, either directly or more likely through their mother, requested that they be given prominent seats in the kingdom when Jesus began to reign as Messiah (Mark 10:40-45; Matthew 20:20-28). Perhaps a mother's ambition for her sons accounts for this unusual request. In any case, Jesus felt the need to rebuke them and to remind them of the need for humility and for lives dedicated to serving others.

John was a man who had a deep attachment to Jesus. He was one with whom Jesus felt he could share his innermost thoughts and concerns. He was thoughtful and firm in his loyalty to Jesus. Apparently, neither John nor James was always mild-mannered.

They seem to have had tempers that could flare up when provoked. They were known as the "sons of thunder." Under the influence and teaching of Jesus, their natural fire and ego drive was redirected. John came to be known as the apostle of love. At the cross, Jesus commended his mother to the care of John, thus reflecting the high degree of confidence he had in him.

Continuing around the circle at the Last Supper, we next find Simon the Zealot. He had been a rebel against Rome. Zealots were those who wanted to overthrow the establishment. "Down with Rome!" was their cry. Somehow he, too, had been caught up by the magnetism of the person and words of Jesus. The man who had been like a flame of fire had been captured by the light of the world and was walking in that light.

Beside him we observe a man of a totally different orientation and temperament, Levi, the tax collector. Levi, or Matthew, as he is better known, was not against the establishment but very much a part of it. This makes it surprising that he is in this company at all. He was one who contributed to the very system that Simon the Zealot hated and fought against. Now, however, they were both changed men. Both had thrown in their lot with Jesus and his company, and so it was that this night they sat together as brothers in the kingdom of God.

Next came Thomas, a man of many moods, ready to die with his Lord, but slow to believe in his resurrection. At one time, when things looked desperate, he showed unusual courage. Speaking to his hesitant companions, he urged them on with the words, "Let us also go, that we may die with him" (John 11:16). Following his special encounter with the Lord after the resurrection, his skepticism was overcome, and he confidently affirmed his faith with the words of confession, "My Lord and my God!" (John 20:28).

About some of the other disciples we know very little. An exception would be Judas Iscariot, who also sat in that intimate circle. How strange to find him there! He was a man who could have been remembered in honor and appreciation. Instead, we think of him with sorrow and remorse. He was the betrayer. He yielded to the temptation of thirty pieces of silver, and in a moment of cowardice and greed he betrayed the Master he had pledged himself to follow.

Though he later deeply regretted what he had done, he could not reverse the events he had helped to initiate. His repentance came too late.

No Two Disciples Were Exactly Alike

What a mixed company there was in the upper room! Peter, a natural leader, sat beside Andrew, a man of quiet decision. James, a man of silence, shared company with John, a man of deep emotional feeling. Simon, a rebel, broke bread with Levi, a man of the establishment. Thomas, a man who offered to die with Jesus, sat next to Judas, the betrayer.

Each of the disciples was unique and different. Here they were all together in one room professing a common loyalty to Jesus Christ. They knew the time was dangerous. They may have been aware that this night might be the last time that they would share a meal together. Soon Judas was to slip out in order to betray Jesus. Then they would be alone, Jesus with the eleven. It was a solemn hour. Into the hands of these eleven men Jesus entrusted his mission, which was God's mission. From this diverse company would come the men who would shortly turn the world upside down. Each man was an individual, but each was destined to make his contribution to the proclamation and spread of the Good News concerning the kingdom of God. These were the men who ultimately changed the course of human history. The influence of their lives continues to transform the lives of each succeeding generation of Christians.

Becoming Jesus' Disciples Today

As twentieth-century Christians, we, too, are disciples of Jesus. The faces around the table are no longer those of the twelve, but ours. As Jesus met with them, so through his Spirit he meets with us. He promised that where two or three meet in his name, there he would be in their midst (Matthew 18:20). As we share his spiritual presence and fellowship, he molds our lives even as he did the lives of the earliest disciples.

In one of his familiar parables Jesus describes four kinds of soil (Mark 4:1-9). The four different soils may be compared to different responses which we give to the Word. Sometimes we are much more responsive to what God has to say to us than we are at other times. The parable speaks of seed sown on the path, of seed sown on rocky ground, of seed sown among thorns, and of seed sown in good soil. Perhaps the parable of the soils was placed first among the parables reported in the Gospels because it deals with what is primary, namely, with our response to the gospel. How we respond to God's call determines the effectiveness of the gospel in our own lives.

The seed which falls on the path is unproductive, for it never germinates. The birds see it and fly down to eat the seed. Our lives are like this sometimes. They are so hardened, so indifferent, so resistant to truth that we completely close our minds and spirits to God's call. The more we hear the truth proclaimed and the more we resist its thrust, the less becomes our power to respond to it. Our sensitivity is diminished, and soon we become spiritually as calloused as the hands of a man who works with pick and shovel. It is not how many sermons we hear that matters. What is important is the degree to which we really "hear" what God says and the extent to which we respond to the message of God to our own hearts.

The rocky ground is ground which has a layer of rock just below the surface. There is enough earth for the seed to germinate, but there is no place for the roots to go. Having no continuing source of nourishment, the small shoot soon shrivels and dies. In this case we respond positively to what we hear, at least initially. The message has the approval of our minds. We grasp it and think well of it. The truth, however, does not sink down to command our wills. We stop short of genuine commitment. Nothing really changes for us—our values, our goals, our ideals remain unaltered. We remain on the edge of the crowd. Are we not all in this condition from time to time? Are there not areas of our lives which we do not open to the probing of God's Spirit? The rocky ground represents the shallow life, and there is still much of that in all of us.

Next, Jesus describes the life that is so crowded with activities and other loyalties that, although the seed takes root, the plant is hampered by the thorns which surround it. Here we see our lives so preoccupied with other concerns that there is not much room left for Christ to work. Sometimes we are so intent on pursuing prestige, power, and money that spiritual concerns must take second place at best. Perhaps we are ensnared by the false glamour of popular recognition or wealth.

The story is told of a young man who was told that he could keep all the land he could run around between sunrise and sunset. He ran and ran and ran, adding field to field, woods to woods, meadow to meadow, always extending the area he thought he could encompass. In a last desperate effort he crossed the finish line just before the sun went below the horizon. He had won. He had become wealthy. He had returned just in time—and then he died. Could it be that the short story describes us? Are we pursuing those things which are a mirage, a vain and foolish fancy? Crowded lives need to become less cluttered so that they may have depth as well as breadth.

Finally, Jesus describes the fruitful life. Here good soil receives the seed and the harvest is thirty-, sixty-, and a hundred-fold. Such soil speaks of an attitude within us that is willing to follow God's truth wherever it leads. It involves a willingness to allow our values to be changed and our conduct transformed. It is a life of adventure with God, open-ended, willing to be led by the Spirit of God.

At various times all of our lives represent each of these soils. Sometimes we are more responsive to God than we are at other times. His promise is that when we do allow his word free flow within us, an abundant harvest will be ours. It is to such a rich harvest of life and ministry that we are called in the world.

GOD CONTINUES HIS WORK IN OUR LIVES

God himself is the source of the maturing process which we have described. When we tap that resource, we need not fear that God will not complete his perfect work in our lives. Such transformation continues after the initial conversion or commitment of a person to Jesus Christ. The good work which God begins in our lives is one which continues throughout our entire lives. Paul speaks with confidence of God's continued work in the lives of the Philippian Christians when he writes, "And I am sure that he who began a good work in you will bring it to completion at the day of Jesus Christ" (Philippians 1:6). The apostle's thought is expressed well by J. B. Phillips' translation which reads: "I am confident of this: that the One who has begun his good work in you will go on developing it until the day of Jesus Christ."

We cannot complete our own lives, certainly not in any spiritual sense. Even as the Philippians did not begin God's work in their lives, neither could they bring it to a satisfactory completion. Paul turns their minds and attention to a loving and sovereign heavenly Father. He is the source of their strength. By reminding them of this, Paul strips them, and us, of all self-glory and of all self-assurance. We are what we are by the grace and mercy of God, and we have no grounds for boasting about any spiritual maturity which we may have realized.

At the same time, by focusing our attention on God and on his sufficiency, Paul has also taken from us any reason for discouragement. Success does not depend on our strength or adequacy. The resources of heaven stand behind us. God is the one who began the good work, and he is the one who will bring it to a successful conclusion. We cannot question God's seriousness of purpose nor his sufficient resources. We can look to God with confidence for strength to bear the unseen burdens and challenges of tomorrow. God has a plan for our lives; and what he has begun, he will bring to a successful completion. Commencement, continuance, and completion—all three are dependent upon the power of God.

Meister Gerhard von Riehl planned the Cologne Cathedral from beginning to completion. The first stone was laid in 1248, the last in 1880, many centuries after the death of the original architect. His plan, however, was carried out from the foundation to the highest arch and the last pinnacle. If human plans can be carried out with such precision, we can assume that divine plans will also be fully realized. Our divine architect lives, and he is at work in our lives in order to achieve his goal and plan for each one of us.

Paul not only speaks with confidence of God's completing his "good work" but goes on to indicate in a prayer what that plan is. He writes,

And it is my prayer that your love may abound more and more, with knowledge and all discernment, so that you may approve what is excellent, and may be pure and blameless for the day of Christ, filled with the fruits of righteousness which come through Jesus Christ, to the glory and praise of God (Philippians 1:9-11).

God's work in your life and mine is an unfinished work.

Growing in Love

The first thing that Paul prays for is that the people in Philippi may grow in love. For Paul love is the greatest virtue. He calls it a "more excellent way" (1 Corinthians 12:31). In his list of Christian graces love heads the list (Galatians 5:22-23). Paul is talking about more than an emotional sentiment. Love is a new quality of interpersonal relationships which grows out of genuine other-regarding concern. He is anxious that the congregation at Philippi may have a unity of mind and spirit in which selfishness and conceit have been banished and where in humility each is willing to "count others better" than oneself (Philippians 2:3). He adds, "Let each of you look not only to his own interests, but also to the interests of others" (2:4).

He cites the example of Jesus who "emptied himself, taking the form of a servant" (Philippians 2:7) and then commends highly the life-style of Timothy who will shortly be visiting them. Regarding Timothy he is able to write, "I have no one like him, who will be genuinely anxious for your welfare. They all look after their own interests, not those of Jesus Christ" (Philippians 2:20-21).

Growing in Knowledge

Paul explains that mature love involves knowledge and discernment. By the first of these words is meant "intellectual perception" and by the latter, "moral discernment." Love must not be thoughtless or indiscriminate. What we love must be determined by what is of value, and what we approve needs to be selected by its inherent worth. Paul says we are to "approve what is excellent." Disobedience to the will of God can blur our sense of values so that we cannot discern with clearness the evil from the good.

Growing in Service

The third element in Paul's prayer may well be viewed as the result which will be realized if love and true knowledge are present in the lives of his readers. Their lives will be filled with the good qualities which Jesus Christ can produce, to "the glory and praise of God" (Philippians 1:11). Paul speaks of the actions which are the inevitable outcome of an inward state of harmony with God. Such a harvest is not the result of our own efforts; it is given by God. Just as the farmer is dependent upon the sunshine and the rain for an abundant harvest, so the Christian is dependent upon the Holy Spirit for a rich and fruitful Christian life. This harvest will manifest itself in our dealings with our neighbors. The purpose of the harvest is the glory of God. God's glory and praise, and not our own, is the supreme goal of all Christian action.

Michelangelo took a mass of shapeless marble and chiseled from it representations of exquisite beauty. We think of the *Pieta* in St. Peter's in Rome depicting Mary tenderly holding the body of Jesus after the crucifixion. The tenderness and warmth of Mary's feelings, as well as her sorrow, are conveyed through the cold marble. Michelangelo's skill makes the stone communicate the emotions he desires. Similarly the Italian artist's able hands shaped the statue of Moses which stands in the church of St. Peter in Chains in Rome. The twists of the beard, the folds of the robe, even the sinews and veins of the arms are skillfully carved into the marble. This is what a great artist could do with marble. What God can do with our lives is much greater. He can make living disciples out of sinners if we will permit him. Remember that there is the potential of greatness in each one of us, rough-hewn though we may come from the quarry of humanity.

What God has begun, he will complete. Paul is certain of this and he reminds the Philippians of it in the verse with which we began our discussion, namely, "I am sure of this: that God, who began this good work in you, will carry it on until it is finished in the Day of Christ Jesus" (Philippians 1:6, TEV). These are words of great assurance. They can be for us a source of courage and faith. God *is* working out his plan in our lives.

We Are Partners with God

As Paul describes God's work in our lives, he makes it clear that he believes that we are called to be partners with God in his work in the world. Such partnership calls for the same quality of obedience which we have seen in its fullest measure in Jesus Christ. In an unusual verse Paul speaks of completing "what is lacking in Christ's afflictions for the sake of his body, that is, the church" (Colossians 1:24). It seems strange to hear Paul speak this way. Does he mean that Christ's sacrifice was not enough for the redemption of the world? There is a sense in which we continue the ministry of Jesus in the world. In identifying ourselves with his person and his ministry, we also are in turn identified by the world as those who belong to the one whom the world rejected. We are told that if the world hated Jesus, we can expect that the world will hate those who take discipleship seriously (John 15:18). True discipleship may, therefore, involve sacrifice and hardship. In our sufferings, however, we are sharing in God's redemptive ministry in the world.

We hear little these days about sacrifice or self-denial. The cross for the Christian should carry a double meaning. Not only does it refer to Calvary where God revealed his love for the world through Jesus Christ, but it should also remind us of a style of life to which we all have been called. We remember the words of Jesus to his followers, "If any man would come after me, let him deny himself and take up his cross and follow me" (Matthew 16:24).

It is our vocation, our calling, our ministry to be participants in the ongoing work of God in the world. We do this with the strength which Christ provides. Paul writes, "I toil and struggle, using the mighty strength that Christ supplies, which is at work in me" (Colossians 1:29, TEV). Mark Hatfield expresses what discipleship means to him as he serves in Washington, D.C. He writes,

> Service to others, solely for their own behalf and even entailing deep sacrifice, is the true essence of leadership and the ultimate form of power. There is a power in servanthood which transcends all notions of power sought after so avidly in the secular political sphere of life.[1]

In his book Mark Hatfield tells of a visit he made in Calcutta with Mother Teresa to a poor Indian family which had not eaten in three days. The mother of this family, when receiving the gift of rice, set some of it aside in a separate dish. She said that she was going to share this dish with another family which had also not eaten for several days. When they left the home, Mother Teresa remarked, "I could have given a double portion of rice, but I did not want to deny this family the blessing of sharing."² It is more blessed to give than to receive. Discipleship means above everything else the giving of ourselves first to God and then to our neighbor. Such giving is the heart of the evangelistic life-style to which we are called.

We Have a Treasure to Share

God calls us to a new life-style that will be shaped and molded by the values and ethics embodied in the Word become flesh. By that Word light entered the world, and we are invited to walk in the light. We are in the world to share this light. It can be compared to a treasure which has been entrusted to us. It is the treasure of the gospel. Paul wrote to the Corinthian church, "We have this treasure in earthen vessels, to show that the transcendent power belongs to God and not to us" (2 Corinthians 4:7).

To many people the word "treasure" suggests ideas of adventure and excitement. Perhaps it brings to mind something like Robert Louis Stevenson's novel *Treasure Island* when Jim, the hero, and the pirate Silver on his crutch discover a cache of 700,000 pounds of gold. The thought of treasure might also bring to mind salvage companies which have been founded for the purpose of recovering treasure lost at sea when ships carrying silver or gold bullion were wrecked by storms off the Florida coast. It has been estimated that one quarter of all the gold and silver ever mined has been lost in sea disasters. Again we might think of the Gold Rush in California in 1848, in the Klondike district of the Yukon in 1896, and in Alaska in 1897. Men risked everything for the chance of instant riches.

Paul says that he has a treasure and that not only he but other Christians as well share in that treasure. The treasure to which he refers is the message which God had given him to share. To Paul it is something of infinite value, much as the treasure described by Jesus is of such worth that, when it is discovered, a man will sell all that he has in order to buy the field in which it lies buried. Jesus, like Paul, is speaking of the treasure of the kingdom of God. The worth of this treasure does not fluctuate with rising inflation, increased unemployment, or the ups and downs of the stock market.

The Nature of God's Treasure

Why is the gospel of the kingdom of God such a valuable treasure? Its value lies in what it can do for us. It can completely change us and make us new. It is like the rising of the golden sun after the blackness of night. The rays of faith and joy which the gospel generates pierce the darkness of doubt and discouragement. It is as if the birds begin to sing again after they have been silent. It can be compared to closed flowers opening and turning their faces to the warm rays of morning. In our lives the presence of God replaces fear with courage, guilt with forgiveness, sorrow with joy, weakness with strength, and despair with hope. It was because Paul had found these things to be true in his own life and in the lives of countless persons with whom he had shared the Good News that he could write, "I am not ashamed of the gospel: it is the power of God for salvation to every one who has faith, to the Jew first and also to the Greek" (Romans 1:16).

To the natural eye, in the perspective of the unbeliever, the gospel is anything but a treasure. To those who turn away it is "folly" (1 Corinthians 1:18). How could it be anything else? The story of the gospel commences in a stable and concludes on a cross. It begins with the slamming of a door at an inn in Bethlehem and ends with the sound of the pounding of nails through the hands and feet of Jesus on Mount Calvary. It has its beginning in a borrowed manger and reaches its close in a borrowed tomb. Is this Good News? Hardly! The problem is that the eye of unbelief suffers from shortsightedness. The story didn't really have its start in Bethlehem nor did it reach its end at the cross. To the eyes of faith the story began ages ago in the eternal plan of God when he loved the man and woman whom he created and made provisions for their redemption. The story reaches its climax not on the cross when Jesus breathes his last but in the glorious resurrection of Christ from the dead. The cross slammed the door on sin, and the resurrection opened an opportunity for all humanity. Jesus opened a door, and at that door he stands and invites, saying, "Come to me, all who labor and are heavy laden, and I will give you rest" (Matthew 11:28). The story does not end with grieving relatives and disciples in the sorrow of bereavement. It affirms rather an exalted and reigning Lord. It is indeed a treasure. The treasure came wrapped in swaddling clothes, but those folds encompassed God's richest gift to humanity.

The amazing thing about the whole story is perhaps the fact that God entrusted the sharing of this Good News to fallible and sinful persons. Paul recognized his own limitations. He can therefore in full integrity speak of himself as an "earthen vessel," that is to say, a clay jar. When we have an earthen vessel, whether for flowers or some other contents, the value lies not in the jar itself but in that which it contains. Paul knew his weaknesses and his limitations. Had he not even at one time been an enemy of the church and of the gospel, having persecuted believers and having them thrown into dungeons? There was nothing here that he could be proud of or boast about.

The same could be said of those to whom Paul was writing. The readers were not the leading citizens of Corinth, the wealthy, the educated, and the powerful. Paul, none too gently, reminds them of this very fact when he writes:

> For consider your call, brethren; not many of you were wise according to worldly standards, not many were powerful, not many were of noble birth; but God chose what is foolish in the world to shame the wise, God chose what is weak in the world to shame the strong, God chose what is low and despised in the world, even things that are not, to bring to nothing things that are, so that no human being might boast in the presence of God (1 Corinthians 1:26-29).

It would be easy for a person to emphasize the weaknesses of the church today. Although the church is not an ideal society perfect in all its ways, it is nonetheless the church of God (1 Corinthians 1:2). That is how Paul addresses the Christians at Corinth in spite of their many shortcomings. Even though the church as a whole and we as individuals are vessels of clay, God has still entrusted to us the treasure of the gospel, a gospel which has the potential of transforming the life of every person who gladly and openly surrenders himself or herself to its power.

The treasure we have is not to be hidden away but shared. The more we give it away, the more we have of it. Its impact on our own lives grows as we share it with others who need the Good News. It is as we walk in the Spirit and are filled by the Spirit that we can best share the love and grace of God with others. Paul writes, "We have this treasure in earthen vessels, *to show that the transcendent power belongs to God and not to us"* (2 Corinthians 4:7, italics added). We have nothing to share that is strictly ours. Our treasure is Christ.

FOR FURTHER CONSIDERATION

1. What gifts or talents do you have which you are using or could use in the service of others? Name some gifts other people you know are using in some form of ministry.

2. Can any job be changed into a calling? If so, how?

3. There is a renewed interest in the expression "being born again." (See John 3:3.) What is your understanding of this term? In what other ways can the reality of which it speaks be expressed?

5
The Church as God's Servant in the World

Jesus often did what was unexpected. He ate with despised tax collectors and with the common people who did not conform to many of the legal regulations of the religious leaders of the day and therefore were regarded as "sinners." Because Jesus healed on the sabbath day, he was accused of breaking the sabbath. Jesus talked with Samaritans, people who were looked down upon by the Jewish community. Jesus gave new interpretations of the law which differed from the oral tradition handed down by the elders. Despite the novelty of Jesus' words and actions throughout his three-year ministry, a further surprise came to the disciples in the upper room. This happened when Jesus got up after the meal, girded himself with a towel, and washed the feet of his disciples. In doing this he illustrated the cleansing which would come to them through his death on the cross. He also set before them in a striking way the life to which they were being called as his followers.

THE SERVANT OF GOD
Why were the disciples so surprised to see Jesus in the role of

63

a servant? They shouldn't have been. His whole ministry had been one of service. Jesus said, "For the Son of man also came not to be served but to serve, and to give his life as a ransom for many" (Mark 10:45). The idea of service or ministry is a theme which is found throughout all of Scripture.

Israel as the Servant of God

In the Old Testament such men as Abraham (Genesis 26:24), Moses (Exodus 14:31), and David (2 Samuel 7:5) were called "servants" of God. More significantly the nation of Israel as a whole was given this title (Isaiah 43:10; 49:3). But to what service was Israel called? In seeking to give an answer to this question, I should like to share an experience which I had in Jerusalem in the summer of 1963. It was my privilege on this occasion to be one of a group of American clergymen and educators who visited in the home of Rabbi Isaac Nissim, chief rabbi of Israel. Speaking through an interpreter Rabbi Nissim asked us the question, "Why have you come to Israel?" One of our company, a Roman Catholic priest, replied, "We have come to Israel because we believe the word of the prophet Isaiah who said concerning Israel, 'I will give you as a light to the nations'" (Isaiah 49:6). The rabbi's eyes sparkled his approval. The verse that was quoted concludes with the statement "that my salvation may reach to the end of the earth." Israel was to be the channel of God's grace, mercy, righteousness, and justice to the world (compare Isaiah 42:1,6,7). Israel was to be God's servant through sharing the Good News of a holy and righteous God who desired that all people should know him and worship him.

Jesus as the Servant of God

As we move to the New Testament, we find that the passages of the Old Testament which speak of Israel as the servant of God are reinterpreted and applied to Jesus Christ. An illustration of this would be found in the temple in the prayer of the aged Simeon who, taking the infant Jesus into his arms, blessed God for having allowed him to see the one whom God had given to be "a light for revelation to the Gentiles" (Luke 2:32).

In the synagogue at Nazareth Jesus read from Isaiah and applied the blessing promised by the prophet to what was happening through his own ministry. This is the passage he read:

> "The Spirit of the Lord is upon me,
> because he has anointed me to
>   preach good news to the poor.
> He has sent me to proclaim release to the captives
> and recovering of sight to the blind,
> to set at liberty those who are oppressed,
> to proclaim the acceptable year of the Lord."
>   Luke 4:18-19, quoting Isaiah 61:1-2

When Jesus had completed the reading, he said, "Today this scripture has been fulfilled in your hearing" (Luke 4:21). Jesus' role was to be the servant of God. The act of footwashing was only an illustration of a way of life. His death on the cross was his final and supreme act of self-giving.

The cross is more than an historical event. It is an eternal reality, for it reveals the everlasting love of God for all people. The event of the cross may be compared to a crosscut made in one of the giant sequoia trees in California. As the tree is sawed, we can look at the place where the cut was made and see concentric rings, each ring indicating a year of growth. No matter where we might cut the trunk, we would be able to count the same number of rings. So it is with the love of God. Our heavenly Father did not love us only on the occasion of the death of his Son. God loved us from the foundation of the world, and he still loves us. He will love us forever. Yet it was at Calvary that he gave his only Son. It was here that he demonstrated the depth of his love.

The agony of the cross reveals both the extent of human wickedness and the breadth of God's compassion. From the darkness of the cross came the dawning of a new day. The shadow of the cross gave birth to the radiance of a resurrection morning both for the Son of God and for all those who through faith in him are born to newness of life.

The Church as the Servant of God

The way of the cross is the way of life for all who desire to follow Jesus. Jesus said, "If any man would come after me, let him deny himself and take up his cross and follow me. For whoever would save his life will lose it, and whoever loses his life for my sake will find it" (Matthew 16:24-25).

If the cross is the symbol of discipleship, there is no room left for egotistical boasting on the part of Jesus' followers. Self-denial is the best evidence of genuine discipleship. In being crucified with Christ we find liberation from the bondage of an ego which seeks to create the world in its own image and to make every other person a satellite moving around that ego. In such liberation lie redemption and the wholeness which Jesus brings. We are God's servants in the world.

In the Old Testament we are told of the ascension of Elijah into heaven. As he left, his cloak fell to the ground. It was the cloak with which he had struck the waters of the Jordan River, and they had separated for him so that he could cross over on dry land. The cloak was a symbol of his role as God's prophet. Elisha picked up the fallen cloak, and with it he in turn divided the Jordan. Those who were with him cried out, "The spirit of Elijah rests on Elisha" (2 Kings 2:15). We might borrow this imagery and say that the servant's cloak that once rested on the shoulders of the nation of Israel was transferred by God to the shoulders of his dear Son. Paul, speaking of Jesus, said that he, "though he was in the form of God, did not count equality with God a thing to be grasped, but emptied himself, *taking the form of a servant...*" (Philippians 2:6-7, italics added). Jesus died, rose from the dead, and returned to the Father. Upon whose shoulders has Jesus' cloak fallen? Who now is God's servant in the world? Has not the servant's cloak fallen upon the church? Jesus said, "As the Father has sent me, even so I send you" (John 20:21). In Ephesians 4:11-12 we read that God equips the saints for the work of ministry. We are all called into God's service. We may be homemakers, teachers, business people, mechanics, administrators, government officials, police officers, nurses, doctors, bus drivers, students, or persons living in retirement. No matter who we are or what we are doing, if we belong to the Christ who served, we are his representatives in the world. Christian service is as diverse as the needs of humanity.

When Neil Armstrong in Apollo 11 became the first man to set foot on the moon on July 20, 1969, he said, "That's one small step for man, one giant leap for mankind." It is time for us as Christians also to take our step. We need to take the stride from status to service, from self-centeredness to self-denial, from privilege to ministry. In seeking to contribute to the well-being and happiness of others we shall ourselves find life's true meaning and fulfillment. In loving we shall discover love. Jesus said, "Whoever would be great among you must be your servant, and whoever would be first among you must be slave of all" (Mark 10:43-44).

The servant's cloak which fell from the shoulders of Jesus when he cried out, "It is finished," has fallen on the shoulders of the church. Perhaps it would be better to say that with nail-torn hands Christ took the cloak from his own shoulders and placed it around ours. How well do we wear his cloak? Those who were with Elisha said, "The spirit of Elijah rests upon Elisha." When the world looks at us, we who profess to be followers of Jesus of Nazareth, does anyone say of us, "Look, the spirit of Jesus rests upon them"?

SERVANTS OF ONE ANOTHER

"What are you doing?" a passerby asked an old man working in a field by the side of the road. "I am planting pecan trees," was the reply. "But surely you do not expect that at your age you will ever get to share any of the crop, do you?" he was asked. "No," answered the elderly man, "but all my life I have eaten from trees that others have planted; so why should I not make some provision for those who will come after me?"

Almost all we have has come to us through the labors of others. We in turn make our contribution to society. That is how life is in the modern world. This principle is also true in the areas of cultural and spiritual values. The ideals we uphold, the attitudes we adopt, and the goals for which we strive in life are by and large all shaped by the perspectives and principles of those who surround us at home, in school, in church, and in society. We in turn by our speech and actions influence the attitudes and ethical standards of our friends.

A realization of this should lead us to ask ourselves whether Christian values really determine the way we live and act. Does, for example, the use of our leisure time reveal Christian principles? Do we exercise responsible citizenship in our community? Do we drive our automobiles in angry, aggressive, and selfish manners, or do we let our Christian values determine that we shall be courteous and responsible persons when we are behind the wheel? We are called to a way of life, not just to an intellectual assent to doctrine.

Seeking the Good of Your Neighbor

The apostle Paul was very much aware of the fact that our lives really do influence others. He gave counsel to the Christians at Corinth regarding a proper Christian life-style for them. One of his first guiding principles was that their actions should seek the good or well-being of their neighbor. Paul wrote, "'All things are lawful,' but not all things are helpful. 'All things are lawful,' but not all things build up. Let no one seek his own good, but the good of his neighbor" (1 Corinthians 10:23-24).

Christian maturity involves responsible action which takes into consideration the welfare of others. As members of the body of Christ we are related to one another. This is why Paul wrote, "Now you are the body of Christ and individually members of it" (1 Corinthians 12:27). The goal we should have before us, said Paul, is "to strive to excel in building up the church" (1 Corinthians 14:12). Individuals are important. They are important to God; they must also be important to us. In a society that tends to treat people as numbers, it is well to remember that God knows each of us by name. We are not numbers to him. We ought not to be numbers to one another. Jesus reminds us that our "neighbor" need not be a member of our own community or even of our own faith. We are called to be concerned even for strangers (see Luke 10:29-37).

The Unity of the Servant Church

In a sevenfold formula Paul speaks in Ephesians 4:4-6 of the new unity brought into the world through the gospel. He speaks of one body, one Spirit, one hope, one Lord, one faith, one baptism, and one God and Father of us all. What Rome with all of its laws and legions could not do, God through Jesus Christ has made possible. That is why Paul can rejoice in Galatians with these words, "In Christ Jesus you are all sons of God, through faith. . . . There is neither Jew nor Greek, there is neither slave nor free, there is neither male nor female; for you are all one in Christ Jesus" (Galatians 3:26-28). The gospel brings people together in a manner in which nothing else does. God changes men and women and alters the relationships which exist between them. Indifference can be converted to concern, and hatred can be transformed into love. This change does not happen through our own resolutions and efforts. Only the power of the Spirit of God can bring about this kind of transformation. Only the gospel can break down the barriers of race, nationality, sex, and social standing which separate us.

Concern for neighbor led to Jewish Christians giving the right hand of fellowship to the recent converts from paganism. It led to slave owners sitting down at the same table of the Lord with their slaves. It led to a growing emancipation of women in the community of faith, thus beginning the process of liberation from the restricted role women played in Judaism and the even more limited dignity shown them in pagan society.

What was the primary problem at Corinth? The basic trouble was that the freedom they now claimed in Christ was "loveless." It was ego centered. It showed no concern for the "weaker brother," for those whose consciences were exceptionally sensitive about unimportant matters. Some Corinthian believers were stumbling blocks to their fellow Christians rather than ladders to aid their faith and to further their achievement of Christian maturity. Paul reminds the Corinthians, and all of us, that we are called to freedom but not to loose living. Ours is a restricted liberty because it is a responsible freedom. We are concerned about how our actions will affect others.

Threats to Unity

In Ephesians Paul reminds us that the work of ministry is for all the saints (Ephesians 4:11-13). Paul ministered in order that the saints might be equipped for ministry. As each believer participates in that task, the body of Christ will be built up. A divided church is an immature church. A united church is a church in which Christ, not any other person, is central. It is all too easy for a church to be divided. Consider the following examples from Paul's own experience.

At Corinth *party spirit* threatened to divide the church. People were saying, "I belong to Paul," or "I belong to Apollos," or "I belong to Cephas," and some, apparently claiming an exclusive relationship to Jesus, said, "I belong to Christ." It seems that the last group was implying that the others did not really belong to Christ. Paul dealt with the issue by raising some pointed questions, "Is Christ divided? Was Paul crucified for you? Or were you baptized in the name of Paul?" (1 Corinthians 1:13). To each question the readers would be forced to reply, "No." Well then, says Paul, let's have no more of this allegiance to human leaders which divides the unity of the body of Christ. We have one leader, Jesus Christ our Lord.

In Galatia *national and cultural differences* threatened to split the body of Christ. Jews and Gentiles were meeting together around the table of the Lord. A debate developed over whether Gentiles should be circumcised (as all Jews were) as a symbol of their discipleship. Paul argued against it, for to him circumcision was a symbol of the law. It suggested to him the seeking of salvation through works rather than through grace.

In Christ all racial and national barriers are overcome. Hence we are no longer "strangers and sojourners." We are all fellow citizens with the saints and members of the household of God (see Ephesians 2:14-19). Therefore Paul can write, "There is neither Jew nor Greek . . . for you are all one in Christ Jesus" (Galatians 3:28). This insight of the first century has yet to be fully accepted and put into practice by the Christian church.

In Colossae *a religious heresy* was threatening to divide Christians. A theological controversy developed in which some refused to give Jesus Christ the central place in their thought. This religious heresy, subsequently called Gnosticism, maintained that one could approach God only through a number of steps rather than directly through Christ. Paul rejected this philosophy and wrote emphatically that in Christ "the fulness of God was pleased to dwell" (Colossians 1:19). In other words he was saying that everything we need we find in Jesus, and we don't have to go to other persons or powers in order to find acceptance with our heavenly Father.

In all of these threats to unity Paul drew the attention of the Christians back to Jesus Christ. In him as Lord, he reminded them, they found their unity and their strength. What Paul did, we too must do. Whenever the church becomes divided, it is because the first place is no longer being given to Jesus Christ. Other centers of interest have developed which have turned away the attention and loyalty of believers. When Christ is given his rightful place, all such secondary loyalties will be set aside and the glory of God and the advance of the gospel will serve to unite us.

Unity Is Not Uniformity

In stressing the unity of the church there is no intention to suggest that what is sought is uniformity of thought, life-style, or worship. Differences need not be a threat. They can be an opportunity for growth. They can provide a chance for mutual enrichment. Look at the work of God in nature. The golden forsythia stands next to the purple and white blossoms of the tulip tree. The chattering blue jay will use your bird feeder along with the cardinal and the red-headed woodpecker. Canadian geese will rest in the same pond with mallard ducks. Everywhere in God's world there is variety. No planet is like any other planet. No star or sun or moon is exactly like another. No heavenly body duplicates our wonderful earth. No blade of grass or sparkling snowflake from the sky is so impoverished that it does not have within itself a touch of individuality from the hand of its Creator. We rejoice in the diversity of creation.

Rejoice, then, that God has seen fit to make each of us different. In the case of some of us perhaps one like us is enough. Paul's concern is not with difference, but he is anxious that there may be in the church a spirit of mutual acceptance, a willingness for each person to make his or her contribution to the ongoing work of God. As J.B. Phillips translates Ephesians 4:2, "[Make] allowances for each other because you love each other."

The appreciation for differences can reach beyond the Christian church. In the concern for justice and social righteousness, men and women of all religious persuasions or political philosophies can find a base for mutual concern and cooperation. The Christian church can show the way by being itself open to the contributions which others can make. In the meantime we can strengthen the unity of the church affirming with Paul that we *are* one in Christ. What is affirmed to be a fact in Scripture we need to make a reality in experience. For this reason Paul can write, "Spare no effort to make fast with bonds of peace the unity which the Spirit gives" (Ephesians 4:3, NEB).

Doing All to the Glory of God

There is a second principle set forth by Paul regarding living as a Christian in our world. It is that we are to do all that we do to the glory of God. Listen to the words of the apostle:

> So, whether you eat or drink, or whatever you do, do all to the glory of God. Give no offense to Jews or to Greeks or to the church of God, just as I try to please all men in everything I do, not seeking my own advantage, but that of many, that they may be saved (1 Corinthians 10:31-33).

Paul speaks in a similar vein in 1 Corinthians 9:23 where he affirms, "I do it all for the sake of the gospel." The vertical dimension gave meaning and thrust to the horizontal aspect of the gospel preached by Paul. His life was a God-centered life. The love which Paul demonstrated to the people around him had its origin in the love which he felt for God and which God himself had placed within his heart.

Self-glory and personal gain did not take the place of the glory due unto the heavenly Father. Paul was God's representative in the world. Since Paul's ministry was shaped by this principle, he even avoided receiving pay for his evangelistic efforts lest his motives should be misjudged and attacked (1 Corinthians 9:11-18). He said he had a right to such material support for services rendered in the spiritual realm but he set aside that claim for the sake of the gospel. He wanted no hindrance to interfere with the free flow of the Good News to his hearers. That which could have been viewed as a valid return for the services he rendered, he set aside for the glory of God. The cross rather than the crown was the symbol for Paul's ministry. It was to this way of life that Paul called the Corinthians. It must be so with us as well. It will be God who will speak his "Well done" if we are faithful, and that reward will be more than enough.

Following the Example of Jesus

A third principle mentioned by Paul which can guide us in Christian living is the advice to follow the example set for us by mature Christians and, as a supreme guide, the example set by Jesus himself. Paul wrote, "Be imitators of me, as I am of Christ" (1 Corinthians 11:1). There is nothing so persuasive as personal example. The Corinthian Christians were far removed in place and time from the earthly ministry of Jesus. They were dependent for examples of Christian living upon visiting preachers of the Good News. That is why Paul was so bold as to say, "Follow me." He did not say this because of egotism or religious pride but from the sheer necessity of the situation. To whom else were they to go to discover what the Christian life-style involved? Note that Paul qualifies his statement in a very meaningful way when he adds the words "as I am of Christ." They were to imitate him insofar as and to the degree that he himself had allowed his life to be shaped by the presence of the indwelling Spirit of God. To the extent that Paul himself was a follower of Jesus, to that degree could he be regarded as a reliable guide for a Christian life-style.

We are not to compare our achievements, whatever they may be, with the accomplishments of others. Our standard is Jesus Christ. When we look at him, we must readily acknowledge how far we all fall short of full discipleship. The name "Christian" implies that we have voluntarily confessed the lordship of Jesus and that we seek to make him Lord in all areas of our lives. He is our leader and guide as well as our savior. Paul puts this idea very dramatically when he repeatedly refers to himself as a "slave" or "servant" of Jesus Christ. The word "servant" is balanced by the word "Lord." It puts in a very clear way what discipleship is all about. It portrays for us what we mean when we talk about a "Christian life-style." It means a life which takes its marching orders from Jesus Christ our Lord. As his representatives, we continue his ministry of service in the world. We do it in his name.

FOR FURTHER CONSIDERATION

1. Is social action a part of the ministry of evangelism? Why have these two concerns often been seen in conflict with one another?

2. Do churches sometimes carry on busywork? Can you think of one or two new forms of outreach and ministry that could be implemented by your local congregation?

3. What is the difference between "unity" and "uniformity"? Can there be a creative use of differences and even of conflict within a local congregation?

6
Human Sexuality

"Male and female he created them" (Genesis 1:27). With these words the Bible begins the story of humanity. Men and women are the creation of God. We are made differently. We are not the same. What are the implications of our differences? Are we rivals or partners? Is there a relationship of domination and subordination respectively? Or is there an intended equality with each sex playing a complementary role to the other?

UNDERSTANDING THE BIBLICAL MATERIAL

When we turn to the Bible for answers to questions like these about the relationship of male and female, there are some very important factors that need to be taken into consideration. If we overlook these elements, we may be confused about what is the biblical teaching on this important matter. First of all, we need to discover the kind of society in which the Bible was written, because this background is reflected in the biblical material. Then we can look at the statement of God's purpose in creation and the effects of human sin upon the fulfillment of that purpose.

A Male-Dominated Society

The ancient world, as is much of today's world, was male oriented. Males played the leading roles in society and were the public leaders in politics, the military, business, sports, the arts, and almost any area that we could name. Women were primarily wives and mothers. Their place of activity was in the home either helping their mothers or grandmothers or else looking after their children and attending to various household duties. This included the carrying of water from the well and often tilling the soil in nearby fields. They were not exempt from hard physical labor. Their place, however, was not in public life. They associated with other women whom they met at the village well, but they avoided contact with the males of society except those of their own immediate family.

The above description of the division of labor need not in and of itself suggest that what men did was more significant than what women did. There is no reason to regard doing business in public places as more important than caring for and nurturing the young. The latter would seem to be at least equally important, if not more so, because mothers were shaping the lives of children, providing for their physical well-being, and giving them their first instruction in life and its meaning. In practice, however, a value judgment appears clearly to have been made, one which even the women shared along with the men. There was, for example, greater rejoicing when a boy child was born than when the infant was a girl. This may have been in part a matter of economics. The girl would need a dowry when she was to be married. The son would help in the family business, would pass on the family name, and would help care for his parents in old age. A boy was considered a special blessing to the family. Mothers appear to have shared the preference for sons with their husbands. In the Old Testament sons are named on genealogical tables, while the names of daughters are often omitted. The family line was traced through the male. The practice of emphasizing males more than females had not changed in New Testament times. Jesus' brothers are named: James, Joseph, Simon, and Judas (Matthew 13:55). Then the next verse, without giving any names, adds the statement "And are not all his sisters with us?" (Matthew 13:56). Were their names not important? Were they forgotten? Why should the brothers be named but not the sisters? There is reflected here the social custom of giving prominence to the males and of treating the females as in some sense second-class citizens.

The inferior position of women in terms of status and privilege which existed in Israel and in all Semitic cultures was even more pronounced in Gentile nations. Consider the statement found in an early letter written in the year 1 B.C. A soldier stationed in Alexandria, North Africa, wrote home to his wife whom he addressed as "sister." His letter reads in part, "Hilarion to Alis his sister many greetings. . . . If thou . . . art delivered, if it was a male child, let it (live); if it was female, cast it out."[1] It was not uncommon in the ancient pagan world for parents to leave unwanted children on the hillside to die of exposure or to be eaten by wild animals. The father's choice as expressed in the letter is a reminder to us of the cruel distinction which existed in the ancient world between boys and girls.

Partners of One Another

In the account of the creation of man and woman in Genesis 2:18 we are told that woman was created in order that she might become man's helper or partner. The verse is translated in *The New English Bible* as follows: "It is not good for the man to be alone. I will provide a partner for him."

Woman, as well as man, is made in the image of God. This implies an equal dignity. That both man and woman share the image of God is affirmed in Genesis 1:27 which reads, "So God created man in his own image, in the image of God he created him; male and female he created them." We need to note that in the above quotation the word "man" refers to both male and female. It is a collective term and includes both sexes. A statement by Paul K. Jewett is helpful at this point. He wrote,

> If Man is male and female by the Creator's decision and act, so that *her* creation is in some sense the completion of *his* creation, then a theology of Man that is male-oriented is surely not one that is based on revelation, one that strives to think God's thoughts after him.[2]

A genuine partnership is intended to mark the male-female relationship. Superiority and inferiority are not the categories which should describe the relationship between man and woman. Where such thinking exists, it needs to be corrected by these and similar biblical passages. Men and women complement one another.

The Fall

Following the description of the Fall, we read in Genesis that judgments were pronounced against the man and the woman. The ground which man cultivates will produce thorns and thistles (Genesis 3:18). These cause his work to become more difficult. As far as the woman is concerned, the following statement is made:

> "I will greatly multiply your pain in childbearing;
> in pain you shall bring forth children,
> yet your desire shall be for your husband,
> and he shall rule over you."
>
> (Genesis 3:16)

How shall we regard these judgments? Are they what God wants to happen, and should we therefore do nothing to try to change these pronouncements? The biblical writers had a high sense of the holiness of God and of the seriousness of sin. They recognized that mankind is sinful and constantly rebels against God. They also saw in human experience suffering and difficulties of various kinds. They tied the two together in a cause and effect relationship.

At the time of writing, man was dominant in human society. Woman played an inferior role and held a lower status. By appealing to the Fall an attempt was being made to explain the way things were. It was simply God's will. By that reasoning one would be in error if one were to argue for equality between man and woman. Such a position would clearly be against the will of God. We need only to follow this line of thought a little further, however, in order to show that it is erroneous. We noted above that there were two other judgments pronounced, one against the man and the other against the woman. After the Fall the earth will bring forth thorns and thistles. The woman will give birth to children in pain. Do we accept these "judgments" as inevitable and therefore not to be resisted in any way? Are not thorns and thistles an intrusion into our gardens and fields so that with hoe and herbicides we seek to remove them? Does not the physician use skill and medicine to ease the pain of childbirth? By the same line of reasoning should we not regard the suggested dominance of man over woman (Genesis 3:16) as an intrusion into what God intended in creation? It, too, is a kind of thistle or thorn, not in the ground but in society. Should not we as Christians be involved in uprooting it?

Perhaps the best way to regard these judgments of Genesis 3:16-19 is to view them as descriptive rather than prescriptive; that is, they express the way things *are* in life, but they do not say that that is the way things ought to stay because it is God's will. God's will in creation was partnership between man and woman. We need to return to God's intention, not to sustain a perversion of that will. This idea has been well expressed in the following statement:

> Subjugation and supremacy are perversions of creation. Through disobedience the woman has become a slave. Her initiative and freedom vanish. The man is corrupted also, for he has become master, ruling over the one who is his God-given equal. . . . Whereas in creation man and woman know harmony and equality, in sin they know alienation and discord. Grace makes possible a new beginning.[3]

Paul Jewett argues in the same manner that man's rule over woman is in violation of God's intent. He writes:

> In this perversion of his true self, he revolts against God and exploits his neighbor, thereby destroying his freedom and living as though he were not a responsible subject. The tyranny of the man over the woman (Gen. 3:16, in the context of the curse) is a notable example of such a perversion of his humanity.[4]

It is true that man has dominated woman for many centuries. Genesis gives us no mandate to continue the practice. We must ask what the original intent of God really was in creation. As members of the "new creation" we will want to seek God's will as he originally intended it to be carried out. Helmut Thielicke has given some helpful observations in the following sentences:

> The story of the Fall does indeed say that the man has superior rank: "He shall rule over you" (3:16). But . . . this is not a commandment but rather a prognostic curse. . . . In this context the fact that one shall "rule" over the other is not an imperative order of creation, but rather the element of disorder that disturbs the original peace of creation. . . .[5]

We need to recover what sin spoiled. We have in Christ already become one. We need to put into practice what God has made true by redemption. As we read in the New Testament, "There is neither Jew nor Greek, there is neither slave nor free, there is neither male nor female, for you are all one in Christ Jesus" (Galatians 3:28). Before God, the Creator, and Christ, the Redeemer, men and women are equal. By the Fall fellowship with God was lost. Redemption in Christ restores the fellowship. By the Fall man became dominant over woman. Redemption in Christ needs to correct this error also and restore woman to her rightful place of equal partnership with man. In the next chapter we shall be discussing the marriage relationship between man and woman.

WOMEN AND MINISTRY

In any Jewish synagogue in Paul's day women did not take part in the public worship services. They either remained in the back behind a screen or sat in the balcony and observed. When there was a time for discussion, after the speaker had finished his exposition of Scripture, the men participated in this exchange but the women were expected to remain silent. Paul's advice to the Christian church of his day was patterned after the practice of the Jewish synagogues in which he had been raised. Women were to ask questions at home, not in the public service (1 Corinthians 14:33-35). Paul had a motivation for giving this advice. He desired to observe local custom and not to give offense by going against accepted standards of behavior.

Paul did permit women to participate in worship either through "prayer" or through "prophecy," i.e., public speech (1 Corinthians 11:5). Circumstances apparently determined when such participation would not offend local practice. In the above passage Paul's chief concern was that the women who so participated in worship be properly dressed. Here he speaks about the necessity of wearing a covering, that is, one which concealed the hair and the upper part of the body, in addition to the regular clothing that a woman wore. Paul's advice is based more on sociology than it is on theology. He urged as a basic principle for worship that "all things should be done decently and in order" (1 Corinthians 14:40).

The passages in the New Testament which speak about women and worship were given in the light of the social conditions of the first century. What offended local custom in the first century does not necessarily do so today. We cannot take social practices, such as separate seating arrangements for women in the synagogue, the necessity of wearing a covering over the head and upper part of the body to conceal the person, and the necessity of not participating in congregational discussion, and then make these sociological aspects of Paul's teaching a final guide to proper procedure for us today. Paul's concern was to apply the gospel to the circumstances of his own day. We must do the same. He did not want to offend social custom lest that offense hinder the advance of the gospel. We, too, will want to be careful not to raise unnecessary barriers to the Good News. We will not, therefore, deliberately cause social confusion by ignoring what is commonly considered right and proper. To imitate Paul without modification, however, is to fail to bring mature Christian thinking to modern living. We are charged with the responsibility of applying the Christian faith and its principles to our own generation, not to the generation of Paul's day.

Women served in various capacities in the early church. They served as deacons (Romans 16:1), labored with Paul in the gospel (Philippians 4:3), and even helped to instruct Christian leaders (Acts 18:26). Just as women were permitted to minister in Paul's day, so they must be permitted and encouraged to minister now. They should serve as deacons, if they have this gift. They should be permitted to distribute the elements at the time of Communion. Their talents should be employed through participation in the public worship service. They should be encouraged to serve as evangelists, teachers, and pastors. Let each serve according to the talents given by God. It is a proper stewardship for the church to discover and to encourage individual talents and to open up doors of opportunity for each person who desires to minister in the name of the Lord.

MALE AND FEMALE SEXUAL RELATIONS

Sex is a gift from God. The Song of Solomon in the Old Testament properly recognizes that romantic love between a man and a woman is good and is something in which to rejoice. The inclusion of this book in the Scriptures is a reminder to us that we, too, need to have a positive and affirming attitude toward sex. Sex is intended by the Creator to bring joy and fulfillment into human existence as well as serving the very important function of procreation. In the sex relationship man and woman become "one flesh" (Genesis 2:24). There is an intimacy in this relationship which transcends all other relationships. It involves the whole person, not just the body. Psychological and physiological union are both present. The psychological factors raise the human sex act to a qualitatively different level from that which is involved in the union of lower species. When sex relations are focused upon the physical union only, the relationship is shallow and impersonal and consequently transitory and unsatisfying.

Sex is an expression of relationship. It is the culmination of a person to person fellowship which is much broader than simply the physical act of union. When real caring is present, then physical union becomes the natural expression and consummation of the oneness which a man and a woman have come to share.

Sex Relationships Outside of Marriage

There are several aspects of sexual relationships which fall short of the "oneness" which God intended for us. Prostitution is an example. The real "psyche" of the partner is not a genuine concern. No lasting relationship is established between the persons involved. This act is an inadequate expression of what sex ought to be. It is a "prostituting" or debasing of sex. To prostitute means to corrupt, to abuse, or to misemploy something. It is a wrong use of sex.

Sexual union involves responsible love. It implies fidelity to one's partner, it is a self-giving to the other in an atmosphere of trust and commitment. As Paul Lehmann has written, it is a transforming union in which we are brought to "human wholeness."[6]

What about the practice of living together before marriage? Many young people are doing this today. They run a real risk. What holds the young people together is presumably mutual attraction. If responsible love is present with trust and fidelity then, as in common-law marriage, to all intents and purposes it could be argued that they are "married," although without benefit of a marriage certificate. If, however, the quality of mutual responsibility and fidelity are not present, then through a hasty decision they may suddenly terminate their relationship. Marriage is a social institution as well as a personal relationship between two people. It involves a public affirmation of intended fidelity. This means that there is built into marriage an intentional stability which can help a couple work out difficulties which arise. A premarital liaison can succumb to a spur of the moment disagreement. It has built into it a potential transitoriness which fails to express the essence of marriage which is an enduring union in which a man and a woman become one. A fleeting or transitory union of the sexes is a perversion of the biblical teaching concerning sex.

Extramarital relations face special difficulties. They are of necessity furtive and create a sense of guilt because they violate the promise of fidelity given in marriage. Even if there is an inclination and willingness to promise fidelity to the extramarital partner, circumstances make it impossible to love "with responsibility." A person cannot make a total commitment to two people at once. The result is an unavoidable psychological tension. The qualities of responsible love and full commitment to the other are impossible under these circumstances. Such relationships therefore fall short of what the Scriptures hold up as God's intent in the union between a man and a woman. That which violates the will of God for our lives is sin. It is not compatible with responsible Christian discipleship.

Homosexuality

In Paul's discussion of sin in Romans 1 he includes homosexual acts. Idolatry was viewed by him as a rebellion against the Creator who deserved worship. Paul then writes:

> For this reason God gave them up to dishonorable passions. Their women exchanged natural relations for unnatural, and the men likewise gave up natural relations with women and were consumed with passion for one another, men committing shameless acts with men and receiving in their own person the due penalty for their error (Romans 1:26-27).

In recent years the public has become increasingly aware that homosexuality is quite widespread and that it is not an isolated phenomenon. How is the church to respond to homosexuality? Is the best approach simply to label it as sin and to cite such passages as Romans 1:26-27; 1 Corinthians 6:9-10; Leviticus 18:22; 20:13? Is this an adequate solution to the problem?

The Cause of Homosexuality

Experts still debate whether homosexuality is a matter of sex hormones or whether a certain behavior pattern is learned through childhood experiences. In other words, is it a physical or a psychological problem? There is no agreement on the reason for homosexuality. Both factors may well play a part.

Some who are professed homosexuals would object to having their life-style called a "problem" at all, any more than heterosexual tendencies are to be called a "problem." From the perspective of Scripture, however, homosexuality is viewed as "unnatural" (Romans 1:26-27). It can therefore properly be called "abnormal" and a "perversion."[7] It is not in accordance with the plan of creation and the plan of the interrelationship of the sexes as described in Genesis 2:24.

Can Homosexuality Be Changed?

According to some reports, changing homosexual tendencies is very difficult and rarely successful. Neither medical nor psychiatric help has shown much success in changing a homosexual's inclinations. If this judgment is correct, then the simple solution of labeling homosexuality as sin may not be an adequate response by the church toward the homosexual. Once we have labeled it sin, do we have anything else to say? In a recent article in *Christianity and Crisis* Peggy Way writes concerning this question, *"We have no choice but to prepare ourselves to work with all people and all possible situations, regardless of our positions on them."*[8] What are some of the ways we can act responsibly toward those who are homosexuals in our families, churches, and circle of friends? What can or should a person who himself or herself is a homosexual do?

Trying to Understand and Help Homosexuals

Most "straights" have a natural aversion for homosexuality, and this has been reinforced by biblical teachings. Our natural aversion will not, however, make homosexuality go away. We need, consequently, to look at the broad principles of Scripture to help us develop a response which is ethically and biblically defensible. Here are a few suggestions which may be a point of beginning.[9]

We need to do all in our power through pastoral counseling, psychiatry, and medical help to aid the individual to move from homosexuality to heterosexuality. We regard the latter as God's norm and the former as a perversion from the natural.

We need to recognize that there will probably be many who will not be changed by such help. In fact, most homosexuals may not wish to change. We do not want to limit the power of God to change people, but we need to be realistic that statistics seem to indicate that some individuals are so constituted that nothing really changes this fundamental orientation to the same sex. In this case we cannot just "give them up" and forget about them. We still have a responsibility to seek to minister to them.

We need to help those with homosexual tendencies to "sublimate" these tendencies into creative and productive channels. To sublimate means to direct the energy of an impulse from its primitive intent to one that is higher in the cultural scale. Here we would urge the person to resist homosexual acts (as unnatural and sinful) and to direct his or her energies toward positive goals. This could be in ministry to other people or in some creative project.

We need to recognize that while we regard homosexual acts as sin, a homosexual tendency in a person may not be his or hers by choice. The tendency itself can hardly be labeled sinful. We need to show Christian concern for the person himself or herself. He or she is a person for whom Christ died. We cannot write off a part of the human race.

We need to remember that we are *all* sinners. Many in our congregations are guilty of heterosexual acts which in the Bible are regarded as sin, namely, premarital sex and infidelity. We do not stop ministering to such people. Do not homosexuals need to be ministered to as well? This does not mean that we lower God's standards and condone homosexual acts. We are called upon, however, to seek to understand those who are caught in this lifestyle and to minister to them where they are. To them as to all others the church must proclaim God's offer of forgiveness and healing. Jesus came not to call the righteous but sinners to repentance (Mark 2:17).

FOR FURTHER CONSIDERATION

1. What inner and interpersonal factors enter into a full and positive relationship between the sexes? Think of this in terms both of marriage and of wider social relationships.

2. Why do women often have difficulty in being called to be pastors of churches? How do you react to this?

3. Why did Jesus relate effectively to tax collectors and "sinners"? Are there any implications from Jesus' life-style for the church's ministry today?

7
Marriage and the Family

The purpose of marriage, as found in the creation account in Genesis 2:18, is described this way: " 'It is not good for the man to be alone. I will provide a partner for him' " *(The New English Bible).* Marriage provides companionship in life in which male and female complement one another. It is a relationship of love and concern which includes sexual union as an expression of that love. The purpose of sexual union is wider than for procreation purposes (see 1 Corinthians 7:3-5). The union makes a man and a woman one (Genesis 2:24; Mark 10:7-8). Marriage provides the family unit into which children can be born and properly nurtured and taught.

The Scriptures advocate the permanence of marriage. "What therefore God has joined together, let not man put asunder" (Mark 10:9). This is the intent of creation. This is the ideal held up before us. Unfortunately too many persons in our day enter matrimony with haste and do so with the thought that divorce is always available if things don't work out. The seriousness of marriage is not fully appreciated. That which is entered into lightly can also be readily dissolved. We need a new appreciation of the meaning of marriage and what God intended marriage to be.

HUSBANDS AND WIVES SHARE SPIRITUAL EQUALITY

We have seen that in the ancient non-Christian world women were second-class citizens. The gospel introduced a revolutionary principle. Women were viewed as having equal spiritual rights with men. We read, for example, "Likewise you husbands, live considerately with your wives, bestowing honor on the woman as the weaker sex, since you are joint heirs of the grace of life, in order that your prayers may not be hindered" (1 Peter 3:7). Women were "joint heirs of the grace of life." This affirmation had implications about their status in the home, not only their status before God. Women were not to be treated as the servants of their husbands. They were to be "honored," not "used" or abused.

The Physical Differences Between Men and Women

In the passage quoted above women are spoken of as "the weaker sex." The reference is presumably to physical strength. This is true in terms of the large muscles of the body, but it is not true in terms of longevity. On the average, women live longer than men. The main difference between men and women is, of course, the fact that women bear children. This is a God-given difference. This function sets woman aside from man. It has no implications about superiority or inferiority. It is a reminder that the sexes complement each other and need each other. For a child to be born, both a father and a mother are needed. There is a difference of function, but both are equally necessary.

The Relationship Between Husbands and Wives

A key New Testament passage which deals with the proper relationship between husbands and wives is Ephesians 5:21-33. It includes the verse, "Wives, be subject to your husbands, as to the Lord" (Ephesians 5:22). At first glance this verse seems to teach the subordination of wives to their husbands. The context, however, suggests that this is not the case.

First, Paul is saying nothing to the wife that he has not already said to the husband. In the verse immediately preceding the one we are now examining, Paul wrote, *"Be subject to one another* out of reverence for Christ."* Spouses are to be subject to one another. Each person is to place the other's interest first.

Second, the comparison of the husband with Jesus Christ as Lord in verses 23 and 25 implies not a relationship of dominance but one of love and self-giving (compare 1 Peter 3:7 with 1 Peter 3:1-6). It stresses, in other words, the servant role of the husband to the wife, not his rule over his wife. Listen to how Paul put it,

> For the husband is the head of the wife as Christ is the head of the church, his body, and is himself its Savior.

> Husbands, love your wives, as Christ loved the church *and gave himself up for her* . . . (Ephesians 5:23,25 italics added).

Helmut Thielicke has interpreted these verses helpfully. He wrote,

> Christ is himself the prototype of the servant (Luke 22:27). . . . From what has just been said it is already clear that what is meant here is something more and something different from a simple relationship of superiority, a kind of "leadership principle" in marriage. . . .
> Their intent is not an objective doctrine of the sexes, but rather an appeal to the husband not to regard and act upon his position as the head in the sociological sense as being one of simple superiority, but rather in the soteriological sense of the imitation of Christ.[1]

Paul was not attacking the place of the husband as the "head" of the home. He regarded his "headship," however, as that of a leader among equals. He interpreted his leadership in terms of responsibility rather than in terms of dominance or rulership. When understood in this way we see that the Ephesians passage is a declaration of liberty for wives and an affirmation of Christian responsibility for husbands. Love and self-giving are the words which best describe the proper relationship which should exist between a husband and his wife. The model for such self-giving is Christ himself.

Paul's View of Marriage

Paul was not a person who undervalued matrimony. It is true that on one occasion he advocated celibacy over marriage (1 Corinthians 7:7, 25-38), but his counsel was given in the light of his expectation that the return of Jesus Christ would happen soon (1

Corinthians 7:29). It was a part of both the Jewish and Christian expectation of the times that the days just before Messiah's coming in power would be days of unusual stress. These would be days in which the saints would suffer persecution at the hands of unbelievers. Paul anticipated such days of crisis. Therefore he wrote, "I think that *in view of the present distress* it is well for a person to remain as he is" (1 Corinthians 7:26, italics added). Paul was suggesting that those who were single should remain single in view of the difficulties which lay just around the corner.

Paul's expectation that Jesus would return in his own lifetime was not fulfilled. Emergency advice cannot be used as a basis for determining how the apostle Paul viewed marriage. He compared it, we will remember, to the relationship between Christ and the church (Ephesians 5:21-33). This passage presents a high and holy view of matrimony.

Paul does view the single state with an apparent degree of idealism. He wrote, "The unmarried man is anxious about the affairs of the Lord, how to please the Lord" (1 Corinthians 7:32). The married person, Paul argues, has his or her interests divided between spouse and Lord (7:33-34). Marriage may or may not be a distracting factor in Christian ministry. One could argue that the married person is in a better position to understand and to be helpful to married people who face the problems which arise in marriage. Furthermore, has not marriage often had a settling effect on young people so that the result has been a more stable life-style and one in which the Lord's work can perhaps be given more attention than it was given before? Paul's judgment at this point might well apply to a person involved in a traveling ministry like his own. It is a statement geared to a specific time and to special circumstances. It is not to be viewed as a universal truth which can be applied without modification through the centuries.

RESPONSIBLE PARENTHOOD

One of the primary purposes of marriage is for children to be born to the union. We read, "Be fruitful and multiply" (Genesis 1:28). We cannot, however, allow natural fertility to run its course. This would be irresponsible. Proper parental care, economics, and world population are only a few of the reasons why such a practice would be wrong. Some means of birth control is needed. The Roman Catholic Church opposes artificial means of birth control but allows for the "rhythm" method.

Responsible Christian parenthood demands that we plan as carefully as we can for the birth of our children. They should come because we desire them, not because they are "accidents." We will love them in either case, but it is much better that children be born to parents who have planned for them. Birth control by artificial means is largely a modern invention. The Bible says nothing about it. It would seem to be presumptuous therefore to argue on biblical grounds that we should not use artificial means in order to prevent pregnancy. Careful planning, rather than chance, should determine when and how many children should bless our marriages.

According to a recent article, about a million legal abortions are now performed every year in the United States. It remains a very controversial ethical issue. When should abortion be permitted and when would it be morally wrong? Artificial abortion involves the destruction of a form of human life. Some would argue that very early in pregnancy the embryo is not yet a human being. If we permit without pangs of conscience the easy taking of unborn human life, how do we significantly differ from the ancients who exposed unwanted babies? What will prevent a future generation from taking the approach that we should remove other unwanted human life from the earth, such as imbeciles, invalids, or the aged?

Abortion is an area in which we need to move with caution. In the case of rape, for situations in which the pregnancy endangers the health of the mother, and in cases where abnormalities in the fetus appear to be present, abortion would seem to be a defensible solution. Certainly a better case can be made for very early abortion than for later ones when the fetus is more developed. The prevention of unwanted or unwise pregnancies is much to be preferred to abortion. Abortion is an extreme solution. It is a decision which primarily needs to be made between a woman and her doctor. Since abortion does have wider social implications, however, all of us need to think about it seriously.

DIVORCE

In America there are now over one million divorces a year.

There is clearly a crisis today in the area of marriage. Divorce has now become so common in our society that it touches the lives of most of us. We nearly all have close relatives and friends who have gone through this experience. How many children suffer psychological damage because of the emotional tearing caused by the break-up of the family unit!

How does the Bible view divorce? Paul will allow it if the "unbelieving partner desires to separate" (1 Corinthians 7:15). If, on the other hand, a Christian separates from his or her Christian spouse, Paul advocates that they remain single thereafter (1 Corinthians 7:11). Jesus recognized that Jewish law permitted divorce, but he said that God did not originally plan it that way in creation. He explains the provision made for divorce by Moses as arising from the "hardness of heart" of the people (Mark 10:5). These words of counsel give very little leeway for divorce. We are caught between two positions, namely, extreme laxity in contemporary culture and a rather rigid code found in Scripture. How shall we then decide our course of action?

Divorce is not the ideal. It is an admission of failure on the part of one or both parties. Selfishness rather than self-giving probably characterized the relationship at some point, and finally the distance between the couple became so great that divorce seemed the only way out. Perhaps the bickering and tension are so constant and intense that this hostility is causing more damage to everyone in the home than a separation would cause. These are issues that each couple (and counselor) needs to weigh. Every situation is unique. Has everything possible been done to bring about reconciliation? Is divorce really the lesser of two evils? To divorce under unbearable circumstances does not make it "right," but perhaps it is the best decision one can make under the circumstances. A strictly "legalistic" approach to the problem is an inadequate solution. The Christian faith is not a legal code but a life to be lived which involves responsible decision making. When love and caring have ceased to exist in a relationship, then perhaps the comment by Emil Brunner is correct when he says, "For . . . the love of our neighbour the only moral thing to do is to dissolve a marriage of this kind."[2] He adds:

Certainly the fact of a divorce is a sign of weakness, and is a specially clear indication that we are an "adulterous generation." But cases are possible where not to divorce might be a sign of greater weakness, and might be a still greater offence against the Divine order.[3]

In that case we can only acknowledge failure and seek God's forgiveness and help. Life goes on and we must continue to live our lives in the world.

At one point Paul urged marriage for single people lest through passion they engage in immorality (1 Corinthians 7:36-37). He has in this same chapter urged that those who "separate" from their spouses remain single (1 Corinthians 7:11). Again we are dealing with what can be called an "ideal." The advice to single people to marry because of inner need may apply equally well to those who have been divorced. The need may not be just for reasons of sexual union but simply because we need love and companionship in life. Once again we are faced with a choice. Should we turn from remarriage because the ideal calls for one marriage only or should we marry because of the deep need inside us which is not being fulfilled? Here Brunner's observation appears to be valid. He writes,

> In spite of our fundamental scruples, actually in most cases re-marriage is the more decent solution, and the one which corresponds more closely to the ideal, than to remain unmarried, not merely for the widowed, but also for the divorced.[4]

If we marry, we may do so with some pangs of conscience; yet perhaps under the circumstances this is for us the best choice we can really make. We don't give up our faith or leave the fellowship of the church because we are not living up to the ideal set forth in Scripture. The church is composed of those who need the Savior and his healing power. The church is also the fellowship which can help find that healing. Fellow believers can embody healing through love and care. We need the church even more when we go through some of these crises, not less.

When divorce comes to people, the role of the church is not to treat it lightly or to condone easy marriage and separation. At the same time the church is not to stand in judgment and simply to condemn those who have gone through this experience. The church must ever speak the good news of forgiveness in Jesus Christ. It must also act out that forgiveness by receiving such persons in love and concern and ministering to them in whatever way possible as they seek to rebuild their lives. We are all sinners. We cannot select one particular problem and say that in this area there is no forgiveness. We all stand under the condemnation of God's law. Yet we all can find in the grace of God the forgiveness which can make us whole and can set before us a new path. This is the good news in Jesus Christ. God can heal; God can forgive; God can rebuild!

THE FAMILY AS A PLACE OF RELIGIOUS TRAINING

Concerning the childhood of Jesus we read, "And Jesus increased in wisdom and in stature, and in favor with God and man" (Luke 2:52). The home of Jesus was clearly a devout one. There Jesus' early religious training would have begun. If it followed the normal pattern, Joseph would have played a major role in that during Jesus' early years. It was demanded by the Jewish law that the father assume responsibility for the religious training of his children. The law stated,

> And these words which I command you this day shall be upon your heart; and you shall teach them diligently to your children, and shall talk of them when you sit in your house, and when you walk by the way, and when you lie down, and when you rise (Deuteronomy 6:6-7).

Since Joseph was still alive when Jesus was twelve years of age, we can safely assume that by the side of Joseph Jesus learned not only the skills of carpentry but also the deep religious heritage of his people. Jesus never refers directly to Joseph. When he speaks of God as "Abba," the Aramaic term for "Father," and does so with evident warmth, trust, and affection, we are probably on safe ground in assuming that Joseph's role in the home had been most positive and that a tender and appreciative bond existed between Jesus and Joseph during the years they had together. Joseph had been Jesus' teacher both at carpentry and in faith.

Religious Training by Others

By the time Jesus was six or seven, he would have been enrolled in the synagogue school to learn to read Hebrew, using the Torah as his textbook, and to study the precepts of the law. Thus his early training would not have differed in any marked manner from that of any other young boy growing up in a devout Jewish home in Nazareth at the time. At the age of twelve he sat with the men in the synagogue on the sabbath day. Periodically he would take his turn in reading the Scripture selection for the day. The synagogue was the center of village life. It provided the religious and cultural link with Jerusalem, the center of Jewish history and faith.

Jesus in his youth was nurtured on the Scriptures. Genesis, Deuteronomy, the Psalms, Isaiah, and Jeremiah were ones that he referred to constantly in his ministry. He met temptation by appealing to them. They shaped his understanding of his own ministry as he interpreted the Servant Songs of Isaiah as being fulfilled in himself. Scripture can mold our lives as nothing else can. We are reminded of the importance of Scripture in the formation of the young by the admonition found in Second Timothy where we read, "But as for you, continue in what you have learned and have firmly believed, knowing from whom you learned it and how from childhood you have been acquainted with the sacred writings which are able to instruct you for salvation through faith in Christ Jesus" (2 Timothy 3:14-15).

The Responsibility of Parents

The responsibility of parents for religious instruction is clearly taught in the New Testament. We read, for example: "You fathers, again, must not goad your children to resentment, but give them the instruction, and the correction, which belong to a Christian upbringing" (Ephesians 6:4, *The New English Bible*). The word rendered "fathers" can also be translated "parents" as it is in Hebrews 11:23. Discipline and love, correction and affection, are both necessary. It is reported that Luther once made the comment, "Spare the rod and spoil the child . . . that is true; but beside the rod keep an apple to give when he has done well." Praise and encouragement are much more effective than are blame and rebuke.

Jesus was God's gift to the world, but in the providence of God he was born into the home of a poor peasant family in Galilee. In that environment, in an obscure and unheralded village, the Savior spent his early youth. Though economically impoverished he immediately became an heir to the rich spiritual heritage of Israel which was channeled to him through the faithful instruction of Joseph and Mary and subsequently through unknown and unsung teachers at the synagogue school at Nazareth. Riches of mind and spirit are not dependent on luxurious surroundings or material wealth. Through the resources of the Scriptures, available to us in our own language in many clear and inexpensive translations, and through the presence of the fellowship of the church we, too, have a rich heritage. Water, however, cannot rise any higher than its source. Nor can we expect to grow spiritual giants if we ourselves remain stunted and immature in our own discipleship. The home, more than any other agency or influence, will in large measure determine the kind of persons our sons and daughters will become. We have been entrusted with a precious heritage and responsibility when by the grace of God children came into our homes. With that blessing has come responsibility. We can become co-workers with God in nurturing our children and encouraging them to make Jesus Christ Lord of their lives. The service of God and of neighbor in the name of Christ and to the glory of the Father is the highest calling to which anyone of us can dedicate our lives. Would that what was said of Jesus might also be said of our own sons and daughters, "And Jesus increased in wisdom and in stature, and in favor with God and man" (Luke 2:52).

FOR FURTHER CONSIDERATION

1. Some people are asking, "Why bother with the formality of marriage? Why not just live with someone you love?" What insight can the Bible give us as to how to respond to this growing attitude in contemporary society?

2. Under what circumstances would you consider divorce permissible? What should the church's attitude be toward divorced persons? How can lay men and women in a congregation help persons who have gone through the experience of divorce?

3. How do you view legal artificial abortion? Why do Christians have widely differing views on this issue?

8
Church and State

The United States of America has entered its third century. The bicentennial year was widely recognized by exhibits, parades, musicals, dramas, books, TV programs, special dress, and a visit by President Gerald Ford to Valley Forge. As we think back to the founding of America, Christians can be thankful for many aspects of this heritage. In America religious freedom was obtained through constitutional law. Beyond that, the high ideals of liberty, justice, and freedom for all were voiced, and America became a model to the world of a land of freedom and of opportunity. It is possible to praise such high ideals and express prayerful thanks to God for those who formulated them and made them a part of the nation's Constitution without at the same time uncritically endorsing everything in America's history, either past or present.

ONE NATION UNDER GOD
A great temptation experienced by some is to identify America as a new "chosen people" of God in which the Old Testament blessings spoken about Israel can be appropriated and applied to

the United States. In an almost unconscious manner, and perhaps even at times quite deliberately, analogies are drawn between America's struggle for independence and the exodus of the Jews from Egypt. England, in this analogy, replaces Egypt as the oppressor. The Atlantic Ocean becomes the Red (or Reed) Sea. General Washington becomes a new founder of the nation as Moses was for the Hebrews. He is immortalized in the vivid reds and blues of the stained-glass windows of the chapel at Valley Forge. While we are accustomed to seeing Jesus, the prophets, or the apostles in such stained glass, here the central personage is the commander of the troops at Valley Forge. The analogy is further developed in the portrayal of Abraham Lincoln as the great emancipator, even as Moses was God's agent for deliverance many years ago. The Declaration of Independence and the American Constitution in their absolute authority take on something of the mystery and inspiration of Scripture.

It is not that analogies are bad. In fact, that is how the New Testament often proceeds, comparing the events of the life of Jesus with Old Testament models. We need, however, to be conscious of the fact that they *are* analogies and that no analogy can be taken so literally that we can uncritically affirm that a political entity such as America is a new people of God replacing either Israel or the church.

We have no biblical or other basis for merging together church and state. All too often this is done in political speeches, sermons, or popular thought. There is a tendency to develop a civil religion that is devoid of a doctrine of sin or judgment. Mark Hatfield has observed that the God of this kind of civil religion is "a small and exclusive deity, a loyal spiritual Advisor to power and prestige, a Defender of only the American nation, the object of a national folk religion devoid of moral content."[1]

The following statement appears to give a rather clear and comprehensive definition of what is meant by the expression "civil religion." The author writes:

Civil Religion is the use of consensus religious sentiments, concepts, and symbols by the state for its own political purposes. It involves a mixing of traditional religion with national life until it is impossible to distinguish between the two, and usually it leads to a blurring of religion and patriotism and of religious values with national values.[2]

There is much to be celebrated in America's history and character without becoming supporters of civil religion. The Constitution and other national documents express the ideals of the founding fathers, for they voice truths which are eternally valid and are in many ways supportive of biblical views of justice and righteousness. Opportunities are open to citizens for education, free speech, freedom of movement, and freedom of religious worship. The Emancipation Proclamation set the standard, yet to be fully realized, of freedom for blacks and, by implication, for all minorities. This freedom is not something merely to be cherished but is a right that needs to be extended to all people. Real freedom includes economic deliverance both for the poor in the United States and the poor of the developing nations of the world. While praising what is good in America her citizens can join hands to correct what is wrong so that the ideals they voice with their lips may become realities for all people. The celebration of past and present moral victories is also an occasion to repent of the misuse of freedoms and of the failure to appropriate fully the rich opportunities offered by the American heritage.

Surely we need to remind ourselves again and again that no political loyalties can take precedence over the primary loyalty which identifies us as Christians, namely, our confession of faith, "Jesus Christ is Lord." Such a loyalty and fellowship transcends all national, racial, political, and linguistic barriers. It will not allow incidental differences of economic, educational, or other distinctions to build walls of indifference or prejudice between Christian believers. All *are one* in Christ.

THE CHRISTIAN AND THE STATE

Various parts of the New Testament speak about the relationship which existed between the followers of Jesus and the Roman Empire. We could begin by citing the words of Jesus "Render to Caesar the things that are Caesar's, and to God the things that are God's" (Mark 12:17). This passage does not give to the authority of the state an absolute divine approval. The verse puts very definite limitations and restrictions upon the state's authority. The authority of the state is limited by the obedience we owe to Almighty God. God's authority takes precedence over the authority of the state. This passage is a repudiation of any view of the state as absolute or as independent of responsibilities to the Creator. Consequently Christians are first and foremost servants of God. They are subject to the state as responsible Christian citizens. In their service to God they are to obey the state as dutiful citizens. At the same time Christians ought constantly to examine the demands of the state to see whether or not these demands further justice and righteousness and are in conformity with the will of God as revealed in the Scriptures. The state is subject to the will of God. It has no independent, absolute claim on a citizen's loyalty. We are not equally citizens of the kingdom of God and of the state. We are first citizens of the kingdom of God and secondarily citizens of the state. It is easy to let national loyalties come before religious convictions. If that happens, the demands of the state are then considered as always to be obeyed without the raising of any questions "for conscience's sake." We do not, however, stand under two equal authorities, namely, God and the state. Rather we stand under *one* supreme authority, the authority of God. As the children of God we have responsibilities to the state even as we have them to our parents, our children, our spouses, our employers or our employees, our fellow Christians, and our neighbors. Our duty to the state is one responsibility among many. In every case our behavior stands under obligation to the will of God and must be guided by the broad principles of Christian ethics.

The Doctrine of Two Kingdoms

Perhaps the Reformation misled Christendom by talking of two kingdoms and of two loyalties, namely the kingdom of God and the state. This idea can be traced back beyond the Reformation to Augustine. In any case we need to examine this way of thinking. The New Testament knows no doctrine of two lords, namely, Jesus and the state. As far as "lords" are concerned, Paul reminds us that we have but One (1 Corinthians 8:6). The doctrine of two kingdoms can be used as an escape. Such a point of view can be interpreted to mean that the state has its sphere of authority and the church has hers. The two are then kept separate. Such a perspective leads to a kind of schizophrenic existence. We leave our Christianity at home when we go to our work. This is a refusal to take Christian discipleship seriously as a total life commitment.

The New Testament recognizes two powers, but they are "the dominion of darkness" and the "kingdom of his beloved Son" (Colossians 1:13). We have moved from one to the other. Both continue to exist. We stand at the point at which they meet and are daily called upon to cast our lot with the kingdom of God. The state cannot be identified with the "power of darkness," but we need to recognize that some of its decisions may well reflect the values of "darkness" rather than those of "light." For this reason our loyalty to the state must always remain provisional.

The State as God's Servant

How then shall we interpret a passage like Romans 13:1-7? Here Paul says that the state is a servant of God and that it demands good and not evil from its citizens. Therefore it should be obeyed. From this passage support was found in the past for the doctrine of the divine right of kings. We need to remind ourselves, however, that Paul does not at this point give a complete and comprehensive guide regarding proper Christian behavior as citizens of the state. The passage is spoken in the context of peace and of political stability. It was expressed at a time when the state had not taken a stand of opposition to the Christian faith. Paul urged the payment of taxes and the showing of due honor and respect to persons in authority. These commands have stood the test of time and remain for us valuable guideposts for responsible Christian citizenship. Paul leaves much unsaid, however. What he does say is no blanket endorsement of the state. Such an interpretation would fly in the face of the Christian confession of the lordship of Jesus Christ.

The State as Persecutor

A few decades after Romans 13 was penned, another New Testament author wrote Revelation 13, and in this passage we see quite a different description of the Roman Empire. It is now seen not as the guardian of justice but as a doer of evil and as the enemy of God and of his people. The beast from the sea (Revelation 13:1-10) appears to be the seer's symbol for the Roman Empire with its claim that people should bow down, sacrifice to, and worship the emperor. The beast from the land (Revelation 13:11-17) has been interpreted as the national priesthood that promoted emperor worship. The state has become a cruel monster, the enemy of the church and of individual confessing Christians. The state has a responsibility from God to order justice in the world. When it acts as did the Roman Empire in its days of persecuting the people of God, it has surely violated any such mandate. When this happens, Christians are duty bound to say "No" to the state rather than to yield to its demands to deny the lordship of Jesus Christ and to give their total allegiance to the state. Such an abuse of political power has emerged frequently in one form or another in human history. All too often the state has sought to make the church and Christians respond uncritically to its demands. Conscientious Christians cannot do this. Their first loyalty is to a higher power than the state. They must first obey God (cf. Acts 4:19-20).

When Conflict Arises

The state must not be allowed to have the last word when it comes to ordering the lives of its citizens.[3] It is wrong to think that the church should deal only with items of personal morality and that the state has the final authority in all public matters. The prophets of Israel recognized that God is Lord of all of life, the social and political as well as the private and personal. If we allow the state full rights in everything it decides to do, we are abdicating our responsibility both as citizens and as Christians. As one author has aptly put it, the Christian way "asks for qualified, not unqualified obedience to the state—an obedience not blind but ethically directed."[4] There is a great difference between "provisional" and "ultimate" authority.[5] The state has provisional authority; only God has ultimate authority.

Regarding the position of the main body of the German Lutheran State Church during Hitler's rise to power, Thielicke has this thought-provoking comment:

> According to the more recently published testimonies of those in power, the reason why the Evangelical church fared so badly under the Third Reich was not just because genuine offense was taken at its message, as many in romanticizing retrospect liked to think. To an equal and perhaps even greater degree, the church was persecuted because there was so much contempt for its pliant and unconvincing character.[6]

In the above quotation the word "Evangelical" referred to the traditional Lutheran State Church of Germany. It stood in contrast to another group of Christians from several German denominations who came together and drew up what became known as "The Theological Declaration of Barmen." The word "Evangelical" is often used in Germany to mean "Protestant" in order to distinguish it from the Roman Catholic Church.

"The Theological Declaration of Barmen" was prepared as a protest against the pressure of the German government to compel the state church to endorse and support without criticism government policies. The Christians who prepared this document met on May 29-31, 1934, five years prior to the outbreak of World War II. They saw the state as posing a serious threat to religious freedom. The declaration was an attempt to urge all Christians to remember that Jesus Christ is Lord and to encourage them to resist efforts on the part of the state to compel them to put the policies of the government ahead of Christian conscience. The following brief excerpt from the declaration will serve to illustrate their concern:

> In view of errors of the "German Christians" of the present Reich Church government which are devastating the Church . . . we confess the following evangelical truths:
> . . .
> We reject the false doctrine, as though there were areas of our life in which we would not belong to Jesus Christ, but to other lords—areas in which we would not need justification and sanctification through him.
> . . .
> We reject the false doctrine, as though the State, over and beyond its special commission, should and could become the single and totalitarian order of human life, thus fulfilling the Church's vocation as well.[7]

The Barmen Declaration affirmed that all of life comes under the authority of Jesus Christ. The state has a restricted authority under God. When the state goes beyond its rightful bounds of authority and demands of Christians that which properly belongs only to God, it is to be resisted. The Declaration was a courageous act. Some Christians resisted the state and were persecuted. Some were killed. Thielicke, who was himself an outspoken critic of the government, indicates in the earlier quotation that the state church was in general "pliant" or yielding in its response to government pressure. Because of his own vocal protests against government policies, Thielicke himself was dismissed from his position as a university professor. He did have opportunity, however, for at least part of the time that the war was on, to preach to large congregations of spiritually hungry people.

The decision at times to say "No" to the state may not result in immediate success coming to the one who makes such a decision. Jesus died on the cross. Mahatma Gandhi and Martin Luther King, Jr., died by assassins' bullets. Did this make their lives failures? Did their deaths prove that they were wrong? Sometimes a firm protest is needed even if only a few feel called upon to take such a position. The stand they take presents an alternative to the opinion of the majority. If the minority view is heard, there may emerge a compromise. Perhaps the state will modify its position. Perhaps the conscience of a greater number of people will be reached. Even if none of these things happen, if we regard the stand which we take to be in keeping with our convictions concerning the will of God, then as serious disciples of Jesus Christ we need to take it even if it proves to be for us a costly one. Persecution and ridicule are nothing new to followers of the One who died on a cross.

CHRISTIANS AND WAR

With each generation war becomes more destructive than before. A recently invented bomb promises to kill people but leave buildings standing. Is this a reflection on what in our day is considered more valuable? Is the loss of art treasures of the past, historic monuments, factories, apartment buildings, and business establishments to be considered undesirable, while the loss of the people involved is considered acceptable? After all, they are "the enemy," a nameless, faceless mass which, because it is impersonal, can be eliminated without too much pain of conscience. Our own personal or natural survival, of course, is the argument which is used to justify the development of new weapons. Such weapons, it is held, will serve to deter potential aggressors. The "enemy" uses the same logic in building its military arsenal, and so the arms race continues.

To pray and work for peace is a Christian responsibility. Jesus said, "Blessed are the peacemakers, for they shall be called sons of God " (Matthew 5:9). The Bible, however, is full of warfare. In the Old Testament God is portrayed as actively helping the people of Israel in battles against their enemies. In some places they are commanded to destroy villages with every living creature in them (cf. Joshua 8:2). Were these the commands of God? Does God desire the destruction of whole villages with men, women, and children? Or should we see in these statements the attempts of early writers to justify the actions of the people of Israel by saying that what they were doing was God's punishment of their enemies? They were only obeying God, they said. We must remember that Jesus said repeatedly in the Sermon on the Mount, "You have heard that it was said. . . . But I say to you. . . ." Our Christian ethic cannot be built by selecting at random from the Scriptures that which agrees with our preconceived ideas and values. If we take seriously the lordship of Jesus Christ, then we must make his teachings our norm. We must judge all else in the light of the revelation which comes through Jesus Christ. It was he who also said, "Love your enemies and pray for those who persecute you, so that you may be sons of your Father who is in heaven; for he makes his sun rise on the evil and on the good, and sends rain on the just and on the unjust" (Matthew 5:44-45).

How can we deal with such an idealistic ethic in the world of real life? We can say it is an impractical ideal. We can say that this applies to a future age when the kingdom will be fully realized. We can say this applies to personal ethics but not to the duties of the citizen toward the state. The readers of this book will have many different views on the subject. This is because Christians through the centuries have wrestled repeatedly with the problem of war and have not been able to come up with a uniform response. We all have to face the issue ourselves and make our own decisions on the matter.

Quakers have traditionally taken a stand against participating in war. Helmut Thielicke, who appears from his writings to feel that the attempt to adopt a totally nonviolent approach in this world is unrealistic, nevertheless has the following observation about Mahatma Gandhi,

Has not Gandhi given us an impressive example of the fact that the symbolical renunciation of force is not merely a "Platonic" act of confession but a factor of realpolitik which can have historical influence?[8]

Many Christians hold to what has been called "the just war theory." This view maintains that Christians should participate in war if the cause is just. Modern warfare and its issues are so complex that it really becomes a question of deciding which cause is more just than the other. Inevitably there will be justice and injustice on both sides of almost every national and international controversy. On this basis many would maintain that World War II was necessary in order to stop the evil brought upon Europe by the Third Reich. Somebody had to stop Hitler.

As Christians debate a proper attitude toward war, there is a need for mutual understanding and for support for those who come to differing conclusions. The right of individual conscience to determine a Christian's decision needs to be maintained. The Christian community should do its part to play a spiritually supporting role both to those who cannot for conscientious reasons participate directly in war and to those who out of a sense of duty and with a clear conscience enter the military. In the meantime dialogue is called for as we seek to discover God's guidance in an area that is critical for the future of humanity.

CHRISTIANS IN A DEMOCRACY

We who live in the United States or other democratic nations have great freedom both to express our views and to influence government. The church can be a moving force for good in influencing both domestic and foreign policy. As private citizens we can let our voice be heard through the ballot box as well as through the spoken and written word. With the greater freedom which we enjoy comes also the greater responsibility. Those who live in more restricted countries or under totalitarian regimes need to bear witness to their faith as well. Their ability to influence government may be considerably less than ours. Nevertheless, the words of Helmut Thielicke to East German Christians remind us that no matter where we are called upon to bear witness to our faith we do not stand alone. He said, "So we Christians in the East are by no means as unfree as we sometimes think; we become unfree only to the degree that we underestimate the possibilities of God."[9] "If God is on our side, who is against us?" (Romans 8:31, *The New English Bible*).

FOR FURTHER CONSIDERATION

1. How do circumstances faced by Christians in the United States of America differ from those faced by Christians living behind the iron curtain? How do their responsibilities as Christian witnesses differ?

2. What are some areas of tension which emerge when we seek to be both loyal citizens of the state and faithful followers of Jesus Christ?

3. Can civil disobedience ever be justified for a Christian?

9
The Holy Spirit in our Lives

There is much interest in Christian circles today in the person and work of the Holy Spirit. The charismatic movement, with its emphasis upon church renewal, places great stress on the Holy Spirit. As we speak about the Holy Spirit, we must realize that we are speaking about God himself.

THE SPIRIT IN THE BIBLE

Not only the New Testament but also the whole Bible speaks of the Spirit. We read about the Spirit from Genesis to Revelation. In Genesis 1:2, for example, we read, "The earth was without form and void, and darkness was upon the face of the deep; and the Spirit of God was moving over the face of the waters." Then in Revelation 22:17 we find the words: "The Spirit and the Bride say, 'Come.' And let him who hears say, 'Come.'"

The Spirit in the Old Testament

In the Old Testament God and the Spirit are identified. They are not presented as two persons or two parts of God. They are one. No distinction is made. The Spirit of God is referred to when the writers stress the activity of God. The Holy Spirit is God in his activity in the world. As the Spirit was active in creation, so the Spirit comes upon individuals to commission them for special tasks or to equip them with unique talents. Joseph, for example, was given his position in Egypt because the Egyptian Pharaoh became aware of his ability to interpret dreams correctly and Pharaoh came to the conclusion that the Spirit of God dwelt in Joseph and that God gave to him special wisdom and insight (see Genesis 41:38). Gideon was triumphant in battle because the Spirit of God took possession of him and gave him courage and military skill (Judges 6:34). Prophecy, too, came through the inspiration of the Spirit (2 Samuel 23:2).

Two passages in the Psalms will serve to illustrate the key thought about the Spirit in the Old Testament, namely, that the Spirit is *God's presence* in the world. They are the following:

> Cast me not away from thy presence,
> and take not thy Holy Spirit from me.
> > Psalm 51:11
> Whither shall I go from thy Spirit?
> Or whither shall I flee from thy presence?
> > Psalm 139:7.

Both passages are in Hebrew poetic form in which parallelism is used. In both cases the Spirit is paralleled by the term "thy presence." These expressions are synonyms. They are two ways of saying the same thing. By "Spirit" is meant the presence of God. The Spirit refers to God as we experience him in our lives.

The Spirit in the New Testament

In the Gospels the same basic idea of the Spirit continues. The Spirit is thought of as God active in the world. By the Spirit, Mary is said to have conceived Jesus (Luke 1:35). By the Spirit, Jesus is anointed and prepared for his ministry at his baptism (Matthew 3:16). By the Spirit he is led into the wilderness (Matthew 4:1), and having overcome each of Satan's temptations he returns "full of the Holy Spirit" (Luke 4:1). He now begins his public ministry. He commences the work for which he has come into the world. An illustration of that work would be the casting out of demons which we are told was achieved "by the Spirit of God" (Matthew 12:28). It is interesting that Luke describes the same event and substitutes the expression "by the finger of God" (Luke 11:20). This reminds us again of the basic concept of the Spirit inherited from the Old Testament, namely, that the Spirit is God's activity in the world. It is his presence, his arm or finger at work.

God works through persons to accomplish his will. When he does so, the biblical manner of expressing this is to say that God's Spirit is present and active, helping individuals in their God-given tasks. This would include the task of preaching the gospel. We can see the close connection between Old Testament and New Testament concepts of the Spirit at this point as Luke includes a passage from Isaiah which Jesus uses in describing his own ministry, namely,

> "The Spirit of the Lord is upon me,
> because he has anointed me to preach good news to the poor.
> He has sent me to proclaim release to the captives
> and recovering of sight to the blind,
> to set at liberty those who are oppressed,
> to proclaim the acceptable year of the Lord."
> Luke 4:18-19, quoting Isaiah 61:1-2.

Gradually in the New Testament we discern a change of emphasis. The Spirit and God the Father come to be distinguished. This seems to develop at the same time as there is an emerging Christology, that is, a doctrine about who Jesus really was. The New Testament church was not satisfied to call Jesus a great prophet nor were its members convinced that the category of Messiah was adequate to describe the one whom they had encountered in Jesus of Nazareth. The Jewish concept of Messiah did not carry divine implications. The Messiah in Jewish thought was to be a man sent by God who would be anointed to be the deliverer of Israel. He would help Israel gain political freedom and would guide Israel into social justice and to obedience to the God of Israel. While willing to call Jesus "Messiah," the church went on also to give him the titles "Lord" and "Son of God."

The Spirit After Pentecost

The church experienced the power and guidance of the Spirit of

God after Jesus' ascension. The Spirit continued the work of God which had been begun by Jesus.[1] Consequently the Spirit was thought of as the Spirit of Jesus and, more often, the Spirit of Christ. The Spirit was sent by the Father and the Son to continue God's work in the world. From this separate idea of the Spirit as the gift of God to the church came the idea of the Spirit as a third person of the Trinity. This doctrine did not receive full formulation, however, until later.

The fullness and richness of the doctrine of the Holy Spirit grew primarily out of experience. That the early church had a rather fluid understanding of the Spirit is evident from the words found in Romans 8:9 where the apostle Paul in quick succession can speak of the Spirit, the Spirit of God, and the Spirit of Christ with no distinction between the expressions. They are used as synonyms. When the church experienced the presence of the Spirit, it was experiencing the presence of the risen Christ, and at one and the same time the church could refer to this as experiencing the presence of God.

Another illustration of the freedom of early terminology is found in the RSV rendering of a passage from Acts where Holy Spirit and "the Spirit of Jesus" are equated. It reads: "And they went through the region of Phrygia and Galatia, having been forbidden by the Holy Spirit to speak the word in Asia. And when they had come opposite Mysia, they attempted to go into Bithynia, but the Spirit of Jesus did not allow them" (Acts 16:6-7).

Finally we may remind ourselves of Paul's statement that "the Lord is the Spirit" (2 Corinthians 3:17). Even as the Spirit is thought of as the presence and activity of God in the world, so the Spirit was thought of by the early church as the presence and activity of the risen Lord Jesus Christ in the world. By the Spirit, Jesus is released into the world, and his presence is everywhere even as the presence of God is not limited in any way in time and space. We can see that the doctrine of Christ closely parallels the development of the doctrine of the Spirit in the early church. In order to maintain a proper perspective, it is well to remind ourselves that we must be careful not to dwell so heavily on the threefold manifestations of God in the world as Father, Son, and Holy Spirit that we fail to remember that God is One and that we have seen him most fully in the person of his Son, Jesus Christ our Lord.

The Holy Spirit was active in creation according to Genesis 1. He is also spoken of as the agent of the new creation, or the birth from above, as described in the Gospel According to John (John 3:7. See the footnote in the RSV.). Paul also speaks of the Spirit as the "Spirit of life" (Romans 8:2). The Spirit brings us into the family of God through his ministry of regeneration. We are then urged by the apostle Paul to be filled with the Spirit and to walk by the Spirit (Ephesians 5:18; Galatians 5:25). The Christian life cannot be commenced, continued, or completed apart from the guidance and work of God's Spirit within each one of us.

The Spirit as God's Gift to the Church

In stressing the significance of the Spirit in our lives as individuals, we need to remember the Spirit is the gift of God to the church, to the corporate fellowship. The Spirit places us into the body of Christ, the church. We are not separated children of God, each one going his or her private, individual way. To be "in Christ" is to be a member of Christ's body. We are members of one another. Similarly the gifts of the Spirit are not given for personal advantage but for the building up of the entire Christian community.

THE SPIRIT'S CONTINUED GUIDANCE OF THE CHURCH

The ministry of the Spirit in the church is rich and varied. The Holy Spirit who inspired the Scriptures is also the one who gives us spiritual help in their interpretation. There are principles stated in Scripture which have implications for Christian life and ethics, the full significance of which have yet to be grasped and accepted. Here the Spirit can aid the church in its search for truth. We are reminded of the words in the Gospel According to John where it is stated:

"I have yet many things to say to you, but you cannot bear them now. When the Spirit of truth comes, he will guide you into all the truth; for he will not speak on his own authority, but whatever he hears he will speak, and he will declare to you things that are to come. He will glorify me, for he will take what is mine and declare it to you" (John 16:12-14).

In our generation the Spirit can still guide us into truth. This truth will presumably not be new doctrine. It will involve instead a deeper understanding of some of the teachings we now have in Scripture with a special emphasis upon their application to daily life. While the slavery issue, for example, was hotly debated in the middle of the last century, nearly all Christians have now come to a common understanding. We all agree that it is wrong and contrary to the will of God. No new Scriptures have been given to demonstrate that fact. Rather, this truth has been hammered out on the anvil of discussion, reason, and the basic principles of sacred Scripture. The Spirit has led the church to a general agreement on the matter. There remain yet many areas where similar fresh insights into the leading of the Spirit are needed in our generation.

Is not the Spirit of God in our day leading us to see that race discrimination is a violation of the principle given by Paul when he wrote, "So then you are no longer strangers and sojourners, but you are fellow citizens with the saints and members of the household of God" (Ephesians 2:19)? The first century had its segregation problem, too. Then it was the Jew who thought himself superior to all Gentiles. With the New Testament as our acknowledged guide and authority, twentieth-century Christians have much less excuse for racial prejudice than did the Jews of the first century in their bigotry toward non-Jews.

We need more guidance in discovering what we as Christians can do about the problem of war. The greatest and most frequent wars have involved nations which profess Christian beliefs. We have sometimes tried to make God support a particular nation. By saying *"Gott mit uns,"* did Germany imply that God endorsed its national interests? Americans print "In God We Trust" on their currency. How well do they live up to this motto in public and private life? No matter what we put on our buckles or bills, God remains above partisanship or narrow nationalism. Patriotism and piety are not the same. Moral values come first. Justice, righteousness, and mercy are the qualities that the prophets of Israel held up as God's demands of a nation. We as the church need to be courageous spokespersons for the same standards. On occasion this may mean that we will say "No" to the demands of the state when its values violate the standards of a holy and just

God. This will be difficult for us to do, and it may result in some people saying that we are impractical, or are idealistic, or else that we lack true patriotism. Discipleship to Jesus Christ demands the courage and the conviciton to swim against the popular current if the current is flowing against moral and ethical principles. We need to seek the guidance of the Spirit of Christ as we wrestle with serious dilemmas such as these. Humility and courage will both be needed.

Equality for men and women in our society has taken giant strides in the last decade, but we still have a long way to go. Women are still viewed as second-class citizens in many areas of life. Many jobs are not open to them. The church is involved in this discrimination. Some quote selected passages from the writings of Paul and thereby keep women from exercising gifts which they may have for pulpit or pastoral ministries. Instead of being in the vanguard for women's freedom, the church may well be the last stronghold in our society resisting the freedom which is inevitable. At this point we need to interpret carefully those passages in Paul's letters which appear to support a restricted leadership role in the church for women. What were the historical circumstances which led to his counsel? Do they still exist today? Are there other New Testament passages which would support the concept of giving women equal leadership rights with men? We discussed this matter briefly in chapter 6 of this book. This area continues to be a topic of earnest discussion among sincere Christians. We need to respect the differing views found among believers and to seek the guidance of the Spirit as he leads us in our efforts to apply the principles expressed in the Scriptures to the new circumstances in which we find ourselves in the modern world.

THE SPIRIT'S WORK IN PRODUCING CHRISTIAN CHARACTER

The Spirit is important for Christians in that it is the Spirit of God working within us that produces Christian character. He enables us to grow into the likeness of Jesus Christ. Paul lists the fruit of the Spirit in Galatians 5:22-23. If these are "the fruit of the Spirit," then we are being told that such character is not the product of self-effort alone. The fruit Paul talks about—love, joy, peace, patience, and so forth—cannot be realized apart from the inner working of the Spirit of God. The Christian life is a progressive life. We do not become mature Christians overnight. Even Paul realized that he had not achieved perfection. He wrote to the Philippian Christians:

> Not that I have already obtained this or am already perfect; but I press on to make it my own, because Christ Jesus has made me his own. Brethren, I do not consider that I have made it my own; but one thing I do, forgetting what lies behind and straining forward to what lies ahead, I press on toward the goal for the prize of the upward call of God in Christ Jesus (Philippians 3:12-14).

This development of Christian maturity involves our cooperation with God. It is God's Spirit that must produce in us these qualities of the new creation into which we have entered through faith. We are not to "grieve the Holy Spirit" (Ephesians 4:30) nor gratify the desires of the flesh (Galatians 5:16ff.). We are told rather to *walk* by the Spirit (Galatians 5:16), to be *led* by the Spirit (Galatians 5:18), and to be *filled* with the Spirit (Ephesians 5:18). Paul writes, "If our lives are centred in the Spirit, let us be guided by the Spirit" (Galatians 5:25, J.B. Phillips). Again we are told, "Never damp the fire of the Spirit" (1 Thessalonians 5:19, J.B. Phillips).

Strength for Service

The Holy Spirit gives us strength for service. The ever-widening concentric circles in the book of Acts, beginning at Jerusalem and moving to Rome, begin when the Holy Spirit is given at Pentecost. No effective missionary effort takes place until the Spirit is given. The disciples had been told, "Stay in the city, until you are clothed with power from on high" (Luke 24:49).

The work of the Spirit is varied. We read in 1 Corinthians 12:4-7: "Now there are varieties of gifts, but the same Spirit; and there are varieties of service, but the same Lord; and there are varieties of working, but it is the same God who inspires them all in every one. To each is given the manifestation of the Spirit for the common good." We each have our individual gifts, given by the Spirit. The Spirit is active in the prayer life of believers. "Pray at all times in the Spirit" (Ephesians 6:18). Again we read, "Likewise the Spirit helps us in our weakness; for we do not know how to pray as we ought, but the Spirit himself intercedes for us with sighs too deep for words" (Romans 8:26).

As we seek to obey Paul's exhortation that we be filled with the Spirit, we need to remember that such a quality of life requires a rejection of a self-centered pursuit of personal honor, power, and recognition. This demands a denying of ourselves and a recognition to a new degree of the lordship of Jesus Christ over all areas of our lives. To be filled with the Spirit is to allow God's Spirit to direct our lives into whatever forms of ministry and service he chooses. While this is the road of self-denial, it is also the way to a rich fulfillment of God's plan for our lives.

Guidance in Conflict Situations

Jesus made a remarkable promise to his disciples when he said, "And when they bring you to trial and deliver you up, do not be anxious beforehand what you are to say; but say whatever is given you in that hour, for it is not you who speak, but the Holy Spirit" (Mark 13:11). Matthew's version reads, "When they deliver you up, do not be anxious how you are to speak or what you are to say; for what you are to say will be given you in that hour; for it is not you who speak, but the Spirit of your Father speaking through you" (Matthew 10:19-20). Luke's version has for the concluding phrase, "For the Holy Spirit will teach you in that very hour what you ought to say" (Luke 12:12).

There is a recognition in this promise that it is impossible to prepare ahead of time for all emergencies. Each situation will demand the response appropriate for that "hour." It would seem that Jesus is urging a continuing trust in the presence of God to help when the hour of crisis and need comes. As Mr. Ten Boom said to his young daughter Corrie in *The Hiding Place,* she would get her ticket for the train when they came to the train station, not before.[2] Jesus does not mean that we are not to prepare ourselves for future events. He does mean that faith in God can remove paralyzing anxiety. God will be with us. He will not forsake us. Meditating on the Word and walking in the Spirit are the best possible preparations for the unknown which lies before us. Thielicke puts it well when he says, "True improvisation means the assurance and belief that after I have done all the careful reflecting I can do God will take over as his own that cause in which I am seeking to serve him."[3]

This promise by Jesus is another way of expressing what we have become familiar with in Matthew's version of the Great Commission, "And be assured, I am with you always, to the end of time" (Matthew 28:20, *The New English Bible*). With this promise the disciples went forth to proclaim the Word in all the world. The presence of the Spirit of Christ with us is our promise, too.

THE GIFTS OF THE SPIRIT AND THEIR PURPOSE

What are the gifts of the Spirit and what is their purpose? They may be defined as special capabilities given to an individual by the grace of God for the purpose of praising God and of ministering in his name. Paul includes among them almost all aspects of Christian service. In the list are prophecy (that is, the clear proclamation of the message of God), service, teaching, exhortation, financial generosity, and acts of mercy (Romans 12:6-8). They also include wisdom, knowledge, faith, gifts of healing, the working of miracles, speaking in tongues, and the interpretation of tongues (1 Corinthians 12:8-10). In fact, Paul sees behind every good work of the believer the impulse and direction of the Spirit of God. The Spirit who is the source of these gifts distributes them to each individual as he chooses (1 Corinthians 12:11). This does not imply inactivity on the part of the believer. To receive the gifts of the Spirit, there needs to be an openness to the work of the Spirit in our lives. This seems to be clearly implied in Paul's exhortation, "Earnestly desire the higher gifts" (1 Corinthians 12:31).

A Scale of Values

By introducing the term "higher gifts," Paul indicates that he does not regard all gifts as of equal significance. Some are of more value than others. Some are more to be desired than others. Paul's primary basis for judging the value of a gift is the degree to which it contributes to the enrichment and benefit of the Christian community. He writes, "Since you are eager for manifestations of the Spirit, strive to excel in building up the church" (1 Corinthians 14:12).

Recent years have seen a rise of interest in the phenomenon of "speaking in tongues." This has occurred in main-line denominations and has not been restricted to Pentecostal congregations. How should we respond to this movement? Tongues are included in Paul's list of the gifts of the Spirit (1 Corinthians 12:10). To rule them out as totally invalid and to forbid them runs the risk of violating Paul's counsel when he wrote, "Do not forbid speaking in tongues" (1 Corinthians 14:39). On the other hand, Paul places some definite restrictions on their use, and he also gives some very specific judgments regarding the relative value of tongues as one of the gifts of the Spirit. For Paul, tongues are primarily for private use as a means of expressing praise to God when normal speech is inadequate to give expression to deep religious feelings. Privately he often used tongues, but in public worship he would rather speak five words which were clearly understood than ten thousand words in a tongue (1 Corinthians 14:19). Such clear speech contributes to "upbuilding and encouragement and consolation" (1 Corinthians 14:3). Tongues were permitted in public worship provided they were interpreted (1 Corinthians 14:5, 27). If there is no interpreter, tongues are not to be exercised (1 Corinthians 14:28). Paul limited speaking in tongues to "only two or at most three" (1 Corinthians 14:27).

Problems Related to Speaking in Tongues

There are a number of dangers to which we need to be alert whenever speaking in tongues is practiced. Foremost among these would be the development of religious pride and a tendency to split church fellowships. Speaking in tongues is not one of the so-called "higher gifts." It is not a sign of greater commitment to God nor an indication of a greater spirituality. Nowhere does Paul say that speaking in tongues is evidence of the baptism of the Holy Spirit, as some maintain it to be. It is one gift among many and clearly identified as one of the lesser gifts. Its primary purpose is for the personal edification of the individual in private worship.

If those who speak in tongues argue that all Christians should do the same, they are making their own religious experience the basis by which to judge others. Such an attitude is a form of religious pride, a sin which the Scriptures often condemn. It implies also a loss of perspective regarding the relative merits of the various and many gifts of the Spirit. Not only is prophecy greater than tongues, but also love is the greatest gift of all (1 Corinthians 12:31; 14:1).

A second danger, which is an outgrowth and result of the pride and judgmental attitude spoken of above, is that the practice and encouragement of tongues in public worship is frequently contributor to congregational disharmony and division. If love ₁ the Spirit's greatest gift, it is equally true that unity is the appropriate by-product of that love. As Paul once wrote, "And above all these put on love, which binds everything together in perfect harmony" (Colossians 3:14). Any practice which leads to division rather than harmony among believers needs careful evaluation and control in the light of scriptural guidelines. If speaking in tongues results in either religious pride or in a critical attitude toward others, it can scarcely be viewed as a positive force for the enrichment of the body of Christ. We therefore need to make our practice conform to the advice given in the New Testament.

This calls for balance. Extreme viewpoints cause friction and break fellowship. Dialogue between differing views needs to be maintained in an atmosphere of mutual respect. Love binds us together as followers of Jesus Christ. Genuine love can allow differences to exist. This applies to both sides of the tongues question. Love is concerned about the spiritual growth of fellow pilgrims. In all of this we can never overlook the fact that the greatest witness to a Spirit-filled life is not a particular gift but a life in which the love of Christ is richly demonstrated. We are urged to "desire the spiritual gifts." In so doing we will do well to avoid imbalance in our Christian lives through giving too much attention to the gift of tongues which in Paul's judgment is one of the lesser gifts of the Spirit.

Tolerance and Mutual Respect

We are not to quench the Spirit or hinder his work and leading in our day. There is need for an openness to the Spirit's moving and a genuine tolerance of the variety of religious experiences and expressions which sincere Christians have found meaningful in their own lives. The charismatic movement can be a significant factor in church renewal today. The test we need to apply to all programs of church renewal is to ask whether through such movements the lives of individuals and of congregations are brought to a greater spiritual maturity and a deeper commitment to the lordship of Christ. That is the purpose of the Holy Spirit's work in our lives.

FOR FURTHER CONSIDERATION

1. Have you seen evidence of the work of the Holy Spirit in your life? In what ways?

2. How do you recognize the presence and work of the Holy Spirit in the lives of other people?

3. What are the strengths and/or limitations of the charismatic movement? How can the church benefit from the positive emphases of this movement and at the same time avoid potential problems connected with it?

10
Ethics and the Future

What Jesus taught in terms of ethics was presented in the light of the dawning of the kingdom of God. He said, "The time is fulfilled, and the kingdom of God is at hand; repent, and believe in the gospel" (Mark 1:15). The coming of the kingdom marked the beginning of a new age. God's kingdom was inaugurated in the life and ministry of Jesus. It will be consummated when Jesus Christ returns in glory and power. We need not wait for that future consummation, however, before we can experience the presence and power of God's kingdom. The kingdom came in a new way with the ministry of Jesus, and it continues to be a reality in the lives of believers through the presence of the Holy Spirit. When we commit our lives to Jesus as Lord, we enter his kingdom (Colossians 1:13; John 3:5). Since the New Testament presents the coming of the kingdom as God's gracious gift in "the last days" (Acts 2:17ff.), it is proper to speak of the entire church age as "the last days." This expression does not refer only to the days in which we are now living, or exclusively to a time yet future. We have since the time of Jesus been living in the last days. The church is the community of the last days, and the Holy Spirit is God's gift of the last days (see Hebrews 1:2).

The study of the end times is called eschatology, a word which comes from the Greek adjective *eschatos* meaning "last." What we believe about the future has a considerable impact upon Christian behavior. We will recall that ethics has to do with moral duty and moral principles. It asks what ought and what ought not to be done. It seeks to determine what is right and what is wrong. Christian ethics asks how we as Christians are to live in the world. When we talk about ethics and the future, we are asking how our Christian beliefs about the future affect our life-style in the present. This chapter will seek to show that there is a very close tie between the two.

THE SERMON ON THE MOUNT AND THE FUTURE

The Sermon on the Mount has as its central theme the kingdom of God. Jesus said, "But seek first his kingdom and his righteousness, and all these things shall be yours as well" (Matthew 6:33). What Jesus taught in the Sermon on the Mount can properly be called "kingdom ethics" or an exposition of "kingdom principles." Jesus affirmed that the kingdom was both present and yet to come. The futuristic element in Jesus' teaching about the kingdom was for many years ignored by biblical interpreters. Albert Schweitzer[1] argued that Jesus' view of the kingdom was thoroughly and exclusively eschatological or future oriented. Jesus taught in the light of the rule and reign of God which would soon break into the world in power and fullness. Schweitzer spoke of the ethic of Jesus as an "interim ethic," that is, one which was intended only for the short interval before God's kingdom would come in power. This interpretation was too limited. It recognized the futuristic aspect of the kingdom but did not give enough weight to the present reality of the kingdom through the ministry of Jesus. Schweitzer's work did have a tremendous impact, however, for no longer could interpreters ignore the futuristic focus of Jesus' ethical teachings.

The coming of the kingdom marks the beginning of the new age. We have already begun to experience the power of the kingdom of God through the new birth and the gift of the Holy Spirit who is called by the apostle Paul the "earnest" (KJV) or "guarantee" (RSV) of our future inheritance (Ephesians 1:14; 2 Corinthians 1:22; 5:5). Since we have already entered the kingdom of God through faith, the principles of the kingdom as expressed in the Sermon on the Mount are for us a pattern for life. It is an ethic for believers, not for the world. Jesus addressed these words to "his disciples" (Matthew 5:1). The Sermon is an absolute ethic, an ideal, which is in this life unattainable. Yet it is an ideal for which we strive, knowing that we will not attain it in fullness until we are made perfect in God's consummated kingdom. "When the perfect comes, the imperfect will pass away" (1 Corinthians 13:10).

We live simultaneously in the old age and in the new. We continue to live in the world and are surrounded by the world's values. We find within ourselves a substantial residue of these values, for we often walk as persons of "the flesh" rather than as persons "of the Spirit." At the same time we belong to the "family of God." We walk in the tension between these two pulls on our lives. Helmut Thielicke expressed this well when he wrote, "The theme of ethics is this 'walking between two worlds.'"[2]

To regard the Sermon on the Mount as merely timeless moral principles fails to recognize that the whole message of Jesus is centered on what God is doing and will do in the world. He has sent his Son, inaugurated the kingdom, and will one day cause his sovereign reign to be fully established. Jesus' ethic cannot be understood except against this background. This is why Helmut Thielicke makes the observation, "Theological ethics is eschatological or it is nothing."[3] Along the same line Carl E. Braaten writes, ". . . the one normative starting point for Christian ethics is the eschatological kingdom of God which Jesus preached and practiced."[4]

JESUS CHRIST THE HOPE OF THE WORLD

The Christian faith is not primarily a faith that focuses on history. Nor is its focus limited to the present. Both past and present are important, but the Christian hope ultimately gives life meaning and purpose. We believe in a sovereign God who is the controller of history and the one in whose hands is the destiny of the world and of all humanity. God's future centers in Jesus Christ.

As Paul wrote, "Christ in you, the hope of glory" (Colossians 1:27).

The great letter of "hope" in the New Testament is First Peter. There we read:

> Blessed be the God and Father of our Lord Jesus Christ! By his great mercy we have been born anew *to a living hope* through the resurrection of Jesus Christ from the dead, and to an inheritance which is imperishable, undefiled, and unfading, kept in heaven for you, who by God's power are guarded through faith for a salvation ready to be revealed in the last time (1 Peter 1:3-5, italics added).

The letter to Titus also speaks of hope and calls the awaited appearing of Jesus Christ in glory "our blessed hope" (Titus 2:13). This assurance makes a great difference when bereavement comes. For this reason Paul reminds the believers at Thessalonica of the promise of the resurrection and says that Christians have a hope which unbelievers do not share. He writes, "But we would not have you ignorant, brethren, concerning those who are asleep, that you may not grieve as others do *who have no hope*" (1 Thessalonians 4:13, italics added).

How Does the Christian Hope Influence the Present?

What we as Christians believe about the future has a very significant impact on how we live in the present. To have a "future hope" is not necessarily to be "other-worldly" and impractical. What we believe determines what we do. It is a false approach to the Bible to make a sharp distinction between the so-called "theological" concerns and the "practical" emphases. The two belong together. The practical instruction of the New Testament builds on a theological base, and the theology taught in the New Testament finds expression in a new life-style. An excellent example of this relationship can be seen in Paul's letter to the Romans. The apostle devotes the earlier part of his letter to a thorough and comprehensive explanation of the way of salvation. It includes justification by faith (1:16) and the future hope (8:18-39). He then comes to chapter 12 and says, "I appeal to you *therefore,* brethren, *by the mercies of God,* to present your bodies as a living sacrifice, holy and acceptable to God, which is your spiritual worship" (Romans 12:1, italics added). The practical encouragement and exhortation emerge directly out of Paul's presentation of

God's "mercies." In other words, God's action for them demands a changed life-style.

Encouragement and Warning

The practical impact of beliefs about the future can have two distinct thrusts, namely, *assurance* or *warning*. First, it can serve to encourage Christians who are suffering for their faith. They are reminded that a glorious future will be theirs. We find this emphasis in such books as First Peter and Revelation. Note how First Peter uses the future hope as a basis for encouragement to steadfastness under trial. The author has just talked about the future hope and then says:

> In this you rejoice, though now for a little while you may have to suffer various trials, so that the genuineness of your faith, more precious than gold which though perishable is tested by fire, may redound to praise and glory and honor at the revelation of Jesus Christ (1 Peter 1:6-7).

Similarly a word of exhortation to remain faithful despite persecution is included in each of the letters to the seven churches of the Revelation to John. This book was written at a time when the Roman Empire had begun to persecute the church. It would be easy for them to pull back from their faith in order to avoid difficulties. Several of the separate letters in Revelation end with a sentence which begins, "He who conquers. . . ." Following this introduction some promise concerning the eternal hope is given. An example would be the assurance given to the Christians at Sardis which reads:

> "'He who conquers shall be clad thus in white garments, and I will not blot his name out of the book of life; I will confess his name before my Father and before his angels'" (Revelation 3:5).

The vision of God in the book of Revelation serves the same purpose. God is pictured seated upon a throne (Revelation 4). This vision affirms the sovereignty of God despite all the threats and dangers which surrounded the lives of the first-century Christians in Asia Minor.

There is a second use in the New Testament of the Christian belief concerning the future. Not only was it employed to encourage Christians undergoing persecution to remain faithful, but it was also presented as a reminder that "we shall all stand before the judgment seat of God" (Romans 14:10). The promises about the future served as a warning against indifference or careless living. God will be our judge. Paul wrote that we are all building on the foundation of Jesus Christ. At the day of judgment our works will be tested by fire. The "gold, silver, and precious stones" will endure the test, but the "wood, hay, and stubble" will be consumed (1 Corinthians 3:11-15).

The fact that we will one day see Christ face to face can have a positive impact upon our lives as expressed in the following passage: "Beloved, we are God's children now; it does not yet appear what we shall be, but we know that when he appears we shall be like him, for we shall see him as he is. And every one who thus hopes in him purifies himself as he is pure" (1 John 3:2-3).

Disobedience results in judgment. In the same book which encourages persecuted Christians to stand firm there is included the following criticism and severe warning:

> "'But I have this against you, that you have abandoned the love you had at the first. Remember then from what you have fallen, repent and do the works you did at first. If not, I will come to you and remove your lampstand from its place, unless you repent'" (Revelation 2:4-5).

Encouragement and warning both emerge from the future hope. The life-style of the early Christians was closely tied to their beliefs about the future.

An Incentive for Action

In recent years the Christian hope for the future has been stressed as a significant force for encouraging present action. This relates especially to social action. Our vision of the future kingdom, when God's reign becomes fully realized, makes us more aware of how far short our present society falls from that ideal. The vision of the kingdom creates in believers a holy discontent with the way things are. We become restless and impatient with injustice, oppression, war, immorality, exploitation, and other similar problems. Our restlessness compels us to become active in changing the world. But our commitment and action do not mean that we will bring in the kingdom. Only God can do that, and he will do it at the time of the appearing of Jesus Christ. We acknowledge that we cannot bring in the kingdom, for Christianity "does not become master of the law of death, of evil, of the demonic in history."[5]

Yet we work for change. Christians have had a significant impact on social conditions when they have refused to let evil continue without protest. Men like William Wilberforce (1759-1833), General William Booth (1829-1912), and countless others have made their impact as they labored for social change on the basis of Christian convictions. In an influential book, Jürgen Moltmann has brought this social concern to the attention of the church in a forceful way. He wrote:

> . . . faith, wherever it develops into hope, causes not rest but unrest, not patience but impatience. . . . Those who hope in Christ can no longer put up with reality as it is, but begin to suffer under it, to contradict it. Peace with God means conflict with the world, for the goad of the promised future stabs inexorably into the flesh of every unfulfilled present. . . . This hope makes the Christian Church a constant disturbance in human society. . . . It makes the Church the source of continual new impulses towards the realization of righteousness, freedom and humanity here in the light of the promised future that is to come.[6]

The vision of what will be makes us dissatisfied with the way things now are. Our future hopes becomes a powerful force for change. This incentive to action was well expressed by the Second Assembly of the World Council of Churches held at Evanston, Illinois, in August, 1954. In what was called "The Message" the statement was made:

> Thus our Christian hope directs us toward our neighbor. It constrains us to pray daily, "Thy will be done on earth as it is in heaven," and to act as we pray in every area of life. It begets a life of believing prayer and expectant action, looking to Jesus and pressing forward to the day of his return in glory.[7]

We are already experiencing the power of the new age. As we allow God to live in our lives, we become his servants in seeking to change those things which are wrong in the world in the light of the way things finally will be. God's promised future becomes our present model. Ultimately, we recognize that God's eternal kingdom will not be established by human hands. It must be God's work. Nevertheless our glimpse of that future glory will not allow us to sit on our hands and just wait for a better day. We will seek to be God's agents in the world to bring this ideal into fuller realization in our own lives and in the life of society around us. Christian ethics and the blessed hope are intimately related.

The Basis for Hope

We can speak with confidence about the ultimate triumph of the kingdom of God because we have already seen God's power revealed in the resurrection of Jesus Christ from the dead (1 Corinthians 15:3, 14-17).

At least three results emerged from the resurrection of Christ:

1. By his resurrection Jesus was shown to be the Son of God in power (Romans 1:4).

2. Christ's resurrection bore witness to his victory over sin, death, and Satan (Romans 4:25; 1 Corinthians 15:54; Galatians 1:3-4; Colossians 2:15; 1 John 3:8).

3. By Jesus' resurrection he became the risen and exalted head of the church who makes intercession for us (Romans 8:34) and who is our high priest before the throne of grace (Hebrews 4:14-16)

Paul speaks of Christ's resurrection as the "first fruits" or sample of our resurrection (1 Corinthians 15:23; compare 1 Thessalonians 4:16). Our bodies will be changed (1 Corinthians 15:51-54). God will give us a new body (1 Corinthians 15:38). The Bible does not explain just what this involves. It affirms the fact of the future resurrection without explaining any of the details. Where human knowledge fails, we can be confident that the power of God will not fail.

There is a new interest in recent years in "the problem of death." Death is a constant reminder to us of our "creatureliness." Every ache and pain has been described as an "acolyte" or warning of our coming death. We are created beings. We are not self-existent. Our greatest weakness and sin is to refuse to acknowledge our creatureliness, our dependence upon God as our Creator. We are all mortal creatures, and therefore we must all face death.

The glorious news of the gospel is that death has been conquered. In Christ we shall triumph over death. Christ died for all of us. We read, "But we see Jesus, who for a little while was made lower than the angels, crowned with glory and honor because of the suffering of death, so that by the grace of God *he might taste death for every one"* (Hebrews 2:9, italics added). As he died for us, so we shall share in the victory of his resurrection (Romans 6:5, 8). As Paul writes:

> I am sure neither death, nor life, nor angels, nor principalities, nor things present, nor things to come, nor powers, nor height, nor depth, nor anything else in all creation, will be able to separate us from the love of God in Christ Jesus our Lord (Romans 8:38-39).

The Scriptures affirm that in the age to come the whole creation will be transformed (Romans 8:18-23). The entire universe will experience renewal along with humanity. There will be "new heavens and a new earth in which righteousness dwells" (2 Peter 3:11-13; compare Revelation 21:1-5).

CO-WORKERS WITH GOD

Encouragement and warning were the two primary reasons for the New Testament emphasis about the future. We have seen that the blessed hope creates in us a proper discontent with the way things are, because in the biblical vision of the future we see the way things ought to be. The biblical teachings about the future were not given primarily in order that we might know ahead of time what events will take place upon the scene of human history. They were given rather because of the close connection which exists between the blessed hope and the life-style to which we as Christians are called.

As Christians we are co-workers with God in his redemptive program in the world. The Christian community at its biblical best is a fellowship in expectancy—eager, triumphant, and united in the task of advancing God's work in the world. Our future is tied to Christ's future. We eagerly await the dawning of God's new day when

> "the earth shall be full of the knowledge of the Lord
> as the waters cover the sea."
>
> —Isaiah 11:9

FOR FURTHER CONSIDERATION

1. What is meant by the expression "Jesus Christ is my *personal* Savior"? Is the salvation which Jesus brings into the world more than personal? If so, in what ways?

2. How do beliefs about the future influence our actions in the present? Can you give examples of how your own life-style is modified by your views concerning the future?

4. How do you interpret the expression "Jesus Christ the hope of the world"?

Notes

CHAPTER 1. IN SEARCH OF A CHRISTIAN LIFE-STYLE

[1] William Stevenson, *A Man Called Intrepid* (New York: Harcourt Brace Jovanovich, Inc., 1976), p. 153.

CHAPTER 2. MAKING ETHICAL DECISIONS

[1] The threefold approach to Christian ethics mentioned here is discussed briefly by Edwin L. Becker in *Responding to God's Call* (Valley Forge: American Baptist Board of Education and Publication, 1970), pp. 15-21.

[2] Helmut Thielicke, *Theological Ethics* (Philadelphia: Fortress Press, 1966), vol. 1., p. 620.

[3] *Ibid.*, pp. 357-358.

CHAPTER 3. A CODE TO OBEY OR A LIFE TO LIVE?

[1] Archibald M. Hunter, *A Pattern for Life: An Exposition of the Sermon on the Mount* (Philadelphia: The Westminster Press, n.d.).

[2] Helmut Thielicke, *Theological Ethics* (Philadelphia: Fortress Press, 1966), vol. 1. pp. 131-132.

CHAPTER 4. CHRISTIAN DISCIPLESHIP

[1]Mark Hatfield, *Between a Rock and a Hard Place* (Waco, Texas: Word Books, Publisher, 1976), p. 26.

[2]*Ibid.*, p. 206.

CHAPTER 6. HUMAN SEXUALITY

[1]For a copy of this letter see Adolf Deissmann, *Light from the Ancient East* (New York: George H. Doran Company, 1927), pp. 167-168.

[2]Paul K. Jewett, *Man as Male and Female* (Grand Rapids: William B. Eerdmans Publishing Company, 1975), p. 20.

[3]Phyllis Trible, "Depatriarchalizing in Biblical Interpretation," *Journal of the American Academy of Religion*, vol. 41, no. 1 (March, 1973), p. 41.

[4]Paul Jewett, *op. cit.*, p. 22.

[5]Helmut Thielicke, *The Ethics of Sex*, trans. John W. Doberstein (New York: Harper & Row, Publishers, 1964), p. 8. Reprinted 1975 by Baker Book House. Used by permission of Baker Book House.

[6]Paul L. Lehmann, *Ethics in a Christian Context* (New York: Harper & Row, Publishers, 1963), p. 138.

[7]Helmut Thielicke, *op. cit.*, p. 282.

[8]Peggy Way, "Homosexual Counseling As a Learning Ministry," *Christianity and Crisis*, vol. 37, nos. 9 & 10 (May 30 and June 13, 1977), p. 123.

[9]The author acknowledges his indebtedness to many helpful insights gained from the discussion of this subject in Helmut Thielicke's book cited in note 5 above.

CHAPTER 7. MARRIAGE AND THE FAMILY

[1]Helmut Thielicke, *The Ethics of Sex*, trans. John W. Doberstein (New York: Harper & Row, Publishers, 1964), pp. 11-12.

[2]Emil Brunner, *The Divine Imperative* (Philadelphia: The Westminster Press, 1947), p. 361.

[3]*Ibid.*, p. 362.

[4]*Ibid.*, p. 363.

CHAPTER 8. CHURCH AND STATE

[1]Mark Hatfield, *Between a Rock and a Hard Place* (Waco, Texas: Word Books, Publisher, 1976), p. 94.

[2]Robert Linder, "Civil Religion and Baptist Responsibility," *Southwestern Journal of Theology*, vol. 18, no. 2 (Spring, 1976), p. 26.

[3]The various Baptist conventions in the United States jointly maintain an office in Washington, D.C., to give public expression to their concern for religious freedom and to speak out if Baptist principles, such as the separation of church and state, are jeopardized through government action. The address of this office is: Baptist Joint Committee on Public Affairs, 1628 16th Street, Northwest, Washington, DC 20009.

[4]Culbert G. Rutenber, *The Dagger and the Cross: An Examination of Christian Pacifism* (New York: Fellowship Publications, 1950), p. 87.

[5]See Howard Clark Kee, *Making Ethical Decisions* (Philadelphia: The Westminster Press, 1957), pp. 70ff.

[6]Helmut Thielicke, *Theological Ethics* (Philadelphia: Fortress Press, 1966), vol. 1, p. 625.

[7]Quoted from Arthur C. Cochrane, *The Church's Confession Under Hitler* (Philadelphia: The Westminster Press, 1962), pp. 239-241.

[8]Helmut Thielicke, *op. cit.*, p. 624.

[9]Helmut Thielicke, *The Freedom of the Christian Man* (New York: Harper & Row, Publishers, 1963), p. 202.

CHAPTER 9. THE HOLY SPIRIT IN OUR LIVES

[1]For a fuller discussion of the doctrine of the Holy Spirit, please see my book *Christianity According to John*, chapter 11, "The Spirit of Truth" (Philadelphia: The Westminster Press, 1975).

[2]Corrie ten Boom, *The Hiding Place* (Washington Depot, Connecticut: Chosen Books, 1971), p. 33.

[3]Helmut Thielicke, *Theological Ethics* (Philadelphia: Fortress Press, 1966), vol. 1. p. 653.

CHAPTER 10. ETHICS AND THE FUTURE

[1]Albert Schweitzer, *The Quest of the Historical Jesus* (New York: The Macmillan Company, 1961).

[2]Helmut Thielicke, *Theological Ethics* (Philadelphia: Fortress Press, 1966), vol. 1, p. 47.

[3]*Ibid.*

[4]Carl E. Braaten, *Eschatology and Ethics* (Minneapolis: Augsburg Publishing House, 1974), p. 105.

[5]Paul Althaus, "Eschatology," *Handbook of Christian Theology* (New York: Meridian Books, Inc., 1958), pp. 104-105.

[6]Jürgen Moltmann, *Theology of Hope* (New York: Harper & Row, Publishers, 1967), pp. 21, 22.

[7]"The Message," *The Christian Century*, vol. 71, no. 38 (September 22, 1954), p. 1123.

Bibliography

Books

Becker, Edwin L., *Responding to God's Call.* Valley Forge: American Baptist Board of Education and Publication, 1970.

Braaten, Carl E., *Eschatology and Ethics.* Minneapolis: Augsburg Publishing House, 1974.

Brunner, Emil, *The Divine Imperative.* Philadelphia: The Westminster Press, 1947.

Cochrane, Arthur C., *The Church's Confession Under Hitler.* Philadelphia: The Westminster Press, 1962.

Culpepper, Robert H., *Evaluating the Charismatic Movement.* Valley Forge: Judson Press, 1977.

Deissmann, Adolf, *Light from the Ancient East.* New York: George H. Doran Company, 1927.

Hatfield, Mark, *Between a Rock and a Hard Place.* Waco, Texas: Word Books, Publisher, 1976.

Henry, Paul B., *Politics for Evangelicals.* Valley Forge: Judson Press, 1974.

Hunter, Archibald M., *A Pattern for Life: An Exposition of the*

Sermon on the Mount. Philadelphia: The Westminister Press, n.d.

Jewett, Paul K., *Man as Male and Female.* Grand Rapids: William B. Eerdmans Publishing Company, 1975.

Kee, Howard Clark, *Making Ethical Decisions.* Philadelphia: The Westminster Press, 1957.

Lehmann, Paul L., *Ethics in a Christian Context.* New York: Harper & Row, Publishers, 1963.

Moltmann, Jürgen, *Theology of Hope.* New York: Harper & Row, Publishers, 1967.

Rutenber, Culbert G., *The Dagger and the Cross: An Examination of Christian Pacifism.* New York: Fellowship Publications, 1950.

Schweitzer, Albert, *The Quest of the Historical Jesus.* New York: The Macmillan Company, 1961.

Stevenson, William, *A Man Called Intrepid.* New York: Harcourt Brace Jovanovich, 1976.

Thielicke, Helmut, *The Ethics of Sex.* Grand Rapids: Baker Book House, 1975. (Copyright, 1964)

Thielicke, Helmut, *The Freedom of the Christian Man.* Grand Rapids: Baker Book House, 1975. (Copyright, 1963)

Thielicke, Helmut, *Theological Ethics. Vol. 1: Foundations.* Philadelphia; Fortress Press, 1966. *Vol. 2: Politics.* Philadelphia: Fortress Press, 1969.

Vanderlip, D. George, *Christianity According to John.* Philadelphia: The Westminster Press, 1975.

Vanderlip, D. George, *Jesus, Teacher and Lord.* Valley Forge: Judson Press, 1964.

ESSAYS AND PERIODICALS

Althaus, Paul, "Eschatology," *Handbook of Christian Theology.* New York: Meridian Books, Inc., 1958. pp. 104-105.

Linder, Paul, "Civil Religion and Baptist Responsibility," *Southwestern Journal of Theology,* vol. 18, no. 2 (Spring, 1976), pp. 25-39.

"The Message," *The Christian Century,* vol. 71, no. 38 (September 22, 1954), p. 1123.

Trible, Phyllis, "Depatriarchalizing in Biblical Interpretation," *Journal of the American Academy of Religion,* vol. 41, no. 1 (March, 1973), pp. 30-48.

Way, Peggy, "Homosexual Counseling as a Learning Ministry," *Christianity and Crisis,* vol. 37, nos. 9 & 10 (May 30 and June 13, 1977), pp. 123-131.

Author and Subject Index

Scripture Index